Carine Silve

Róisín Bán
Contents

Róisín Bán: First published in Great Britain
by Leeds Irish Health and Homes
Unit 5, Gemini Park, Sheepscar Way,
Leeds LS7 3JB. Tel: 0044 (0)113 2625614
www.lihh.org
www.roisinban.org
© Leeds Irish Health and Homes.

Contemporary photographs © Corinne Silva, 2005.
Foreword © Dermot Bolger, 2006.
Introduction © Brendan McGowan, 2005.
Poem 'A Deserted Townland' © Bernard Dwyer.
Reproduction of archive images with kind permission of:
Leeds Libraries and Information Services, The National
Archives, Danny and Helen Kennally, Eileen Laurent,
Terry O'Neill, Jason Rooney and Mrs. May.

Book design: Andy Edwards Design, Leeds.
Print and reprographics: Jigsaw, Leeds.
Interviews and editing: Corinne Silva and Rosemary Francis.
C-Type photographic printing: Charlie Meecham.
Black and white photographic printing: John Angerson.

ISBN 0-9552529-0-3
(978-0-9552529-0-7)

Acknowledgements:
We offer our sincere thanks to everyone who
contributed to the project through their interviews
and photographs. This work would not have been
possible without the funding provided by the Home
Office Connecting Communities Fund and the
Heritage Lottery Fund.

Ant Hanlon:
I am immensely grateful to Brendan McGowan for
his contribution. Also to Andy Edwards Design who
continue to provide inspiration and artistic direction
for us at Leeds Irish Health and Homes. I would also
like to thank those people who have contributed both
in money and kind along the way who are too
numerous to mention.

Corinne Silva:
Thank you to Ant Hanlon and all the staff at Leeds
Irish Health and Homes, Andy Edwards, Justin Brooke,
Brendan McGowan, Teresa O'Driscoll, Katie Lister,
Casey Orr, Victor de Jesus, Kathrin Ollroge, Anna
Dunne, Alex Coley, Martin Patterson, Leeds Irish
Centre, Danny and Helen Kennally for all your advice,
support and enthusiasm.

Special thanks to John Angerson, Eric Nicholson
and Rosemary Francis for giving so much of your time,
expertise and support.

Róisín Bán
Introduction

The idea for Róisín Bán came about because my organisation was meeting Irish people whose stories of travel, loss, opportunity and paradoxical emotions were important tales of an emigrant community. Their journeys are very rarely captured when looking at immigration patterns and history within the UK context.

As the son of Irish parents, my identity has often been fragmented throughout the years by whether being Irish was right at the time; it was something my white skin and lack of accent could hide, but nevertheless it was an inherent part of me, leading to many clashes of conscience. The 'Troubles' led to, like many Muslim people today, the risk of you denying or apologising for your Irishness just because you were and not through any shared culpability. The jokes made you both angry and sad. You either hit back or stayed quiet. Johnny Giles, George Best, Steve Heighway, Liam Brady and Ray Houghton's winning goal against England in 1988 raised your national pride. The Pogues'

passion and belief in their right to be proud of their heritage gave young people like me an opportunity to honour roots which may have been pushed to the back. We are a mixture of many experiences and identities, but what is apparent throughout this work is that being an Irish person in Leeds has a resonance with many other migrant communities and is a story that needs telling and preserving. That is what we have tried to do throughout Róisín Bán.

I would like to commend Corinne Silva, the co-ordinator of this project. Her eye for detail and her ability to let people tell their stories in words and pictures is immense and I'm sure you will see and hear great things about her in the future. I hope you enjoy the work and by all means, share the experience with your friends.

Ant Hanlon
Director
Leeds Irish Health & Homes

Foreword
Dermot Bolger

The story of my extended family is probably an average story of the generation born in the same decade as the Irish State. My father was born into a family of seven in Wexford Town, my mother into a family of eleven on a farm in Annyalla near Castleblaney in Monaghan. With the exception of one sibling who tragically died in each family and another who inherited the house, all the other brothers and sisters in each family were forced to emigrate, although one uncle managed to keep his family in Ireland while frequently working abroad, mainly in English car plants. I possess only a few Irish-born cousins but far more with Luton, Coventry, Leicester, Wolverhampton and London accents. Indeed my sole reason for possessing a Dublin accent is that my father, thankfully still alive and enjoying his eighty-seventh year, was a sailor who emigrated twice a week for forty-four years, including sailing through the war on those vital small Irish ships that, although officially neutral, were frequently bombed.

As shown by the collected stories and photographs taken by Corinne Silva within the pages of Róisín Bán and by Brendan McGowan's superb historical survey of Irish emigration to Leeds, the story of my extended family is not exceptional. Eighty percent of Irish children born between 1931 and 1941 had to emigrate. From any group of forty pupils in a village classroom in 1950 only eight could expect to live as adults in Ireland. The others left because, quite simply, there was nothing for them here. They left to the unspoken relief of government ministers who knew that emigration was a safety valve on social unrest, sluicing away the disaffected and allowing the government not to tackle fundamental problems within the Irish State. They left to the gain of successive Ministers for Finance, who were able to factor emigrants' remittances as an invisible export into their budgets. All those ten-shilling notes sent home to Mayo and elsewhere from Leeds counted for more than loose change. At a time of low economic output during the height of Ireland's slump, emigrants were subsidising the Irish economy by the equivalent of over nine hundred and fifty million euros every year in today's money.

Yet despite providing this huge subsidy, they also left with their Taoiseach's disdain ringing in their ears. Annoyed at their greedy abandonment of his self-proclaimed paradise of 'frugal comfort', De Valera declared that: "Work is available at home, and in conditions infinitely better from the point of both health and morals...There is no doubt that many of those who emigrate could find employment at home at as good, or better, wages—and with living conditions far better—than they find in Britain."

De Valera could tell better fairy tales than his wife, who published several books of them. But surely even he blushed at spouting such rubbish when agricultural workers in the West of Ireland worked from 6 am until 6 pm—often sleeping in outhouses that would look uncannily familiar to migrant workers arriving here from Moldova today. Apprentices within C.I.E. and elsewhere were automatically let go on the day they qualified and would have to be paid a proper wage. Like thousands of others they took the boat and—apart from their remittances which invisibly kept Ireland afloat—were written from history.

As Joseph O'Connor noted, 'At the heart of the Irish emigrant experience there is a caution, a refusal to speak, a fear of the world.' This caution meant that the emigrant experience was only represented in a few works like Donal MacAmhlaigh's superb *Dialann Deorai (Confessions of an Irish Navvy)* and Tom Murphy's *A Whistle in the Dark*, which was vehemently rejected by Earnest Blythe in the Abbey Theatre who refused to accept that such people existed.

Novelists like James Ryan (*Home from England*) and Philip Casey (*The Water Star*), along with such books as Catherine Dunne's brilliant set of interviews made with Irish people growing old in London in *An Unconsidered People*, have begun to break that silence. And equally, it seems to me, the photographs and memories contained within the pages of Róisín Bán are an integral and vital part of this process of reclaiming that lost past and giving voice to a generation of emigrants written out of Irish history.

However Róisín Bán is not just the story of one generation. In Corinne Silva's astutely observed photographs—culminating in a Yorkshire rose being carried to the top of Croagh Patrick—is an ongoing story of families who made their home around Leeds, of children growing up with Yorkshire accents and Irish faces, of people who sometimes feel that they either have no home or else have two homes calling them in different ways. Of the earlier images retrieved here, none is more stark than

the photograph of thirteen men posing at Tallaghan Bawn, Geesala, Co Mayo in 1957, and the knowledge that, within one year of it being taken, every man had emigrated. But they did not disappear into thin air. They—and thousands of others—made new lives for themselves, they opened the Irish centres and boxing clubs seen in these photographs. They frequented Irish ballrooms and sought out the sort of partner whom they would have married at home. They carried their Ireland within them. They did not step out of Irish life, but broadened out Irish life to encompass the streets of Leeds, Halifax, Huddersfield and dozens of English and Scottish towns.

Too often in the past, the old family photographs, seen here of Brass Street or of First Communions and Irish bars, were lost amid the debris of life, either burnt or thrown in plastic sacks onto skips. One of the secrets of photography is that it steals a moment from time and cheats the headlong rush of years. Róisín Bán reclaims some of those lives which were nearly forgotten and gives expression to a generation growing old in exile—often unable to relate to an Ireland that shipped them away and shows little appetite for their return. But the book also celebrates the vibrant legacy of the Irish who settled in Leeds. Corinne Silva's photographs and interviews explore a cultural and physical journey between Mayo and Leeds. They reflect on the Irish generations who grew up, and continue to grow, in Leeds. Their lives are now both an integral part of the ongoing story of Yorkshire and the ongoing story of those Irish townlands from which their parents and grandparents set out with suitcases and dreams.

Dermot Bolger

Dermot Bolger
is an Irish poet, novelist and playwright whose books include *The Journey Home* and *The Family on Paradise Pier*.

Emigrants return to the
USA from Shannon Airport
after visiting home.
(1968)

The Emigrant

The car is yoked before the door,
And time will let us dance no more.
Come, fiddler, now, and play for me
Farewell to barn and stack and tree.
Today the fields looked wet and cold,
The mearings gapped, the cattle old.
Things are not what they used to be
Farewell to barn and stack and tree.

I go, without the heart to go,
To kindred that I hardly know.
Drink, neighbour, drink a health with me
Farewell to barn and stack and tree.

Five hours will see me stowed aboard,
the gangplank up, the ship unmoored.
Christ grant no tempest shakes the sea
Farewell to barn and stack and tree.

Joseph Campbell,
Irishry (1913)

Irish emigration:
an introduction

1
Emigration denotes the act of leaving one's native country to settle elsewhere. An emigrant is someone who intends to reside permanently abroad, not a casual visitor or traveller. Emigration means 'out-migration'.

2
P.J. Drudy, 'Migration between Ireland & England Since Independence', in P.J. Drudy (ed.), *Irish Studies 5: Ireland and Britain Since 1922,* 1986.

Emigration is a common theme throughout Irish history, one that has touched almost every family in Ireland.[1] Over the course of the last two centuries in particular, Ireland has borne witness to the departure of entire generations of her people. It is estimated that between 1801 and 1921 almost 8 million people departed Irish shores for new lives, mainly in the United States and Great Britain.[2] From the 1930s onwards, England rather than the United States became the destination of choice for Irish emigrants. By 1971, the Irish constituted the largest migrant grouping in Britain. The 1971 Census of Population of England and Wales recorded 957,830 (958,000) persons born on the island of Ireland.

Today the Irish diaspora, that is Irish emigrants and their descendants, greatly outnumbers the actual population of Ireland. It is estimated that the figure for the Irish diaspora or Irish global community lies somewhere in the region of 85 million people, 44 million of whom are in the United States, 8 million of whom reside in Britain, 7 million in Australia and 4 million in Canada. This is all the more phenomenal when you consider that the current population of Ireland is approximately 5.5 million, north and south. Although the impact of emigration on Ireland and Irish society can never be fully appreciated, it has been a dynamic force in shaping Ireland's social fabric and has been a central thread of the relationship between Ireland and the rest of the world. The aim of this brief introduction is two-fold. Firstly, it is to provide an overview of Irish emigration. It will provide some answers to the 'when', 'who' and 'why' of Irish emigration. The second aim is to provide a contextual background to the history of the Irish community in Leeds.

Irish migration:
an overview

3
Immigration denotes the act of moving into or settling in another country, temporarily or permanently. An immigrant is someone who intends to reside permanently, not a casual visitor or traveller. Immigration means 'in-migration'.

4
C. J. Houston & W. J. Smyth, 'The Irish Diaspora: Emigration to the New World, 1720-1920', in B. J. Graham & L. J. Proudfoot (eds.), *An Historical Geography of Ireland*, 1993.

5
R. F. Foster, *Modern Ireland*, 1600–1972, 1989.

6
C. J. Houston & W. J. Smyth, 'The Irish Diaspora: Emigration to the New World, 1720–1920', in B. J. Graham & L. J. Proudfoot (eds.), *An Historical Geography of Ireland*, 1993.

7
Russell King, Ian Shuttleworth & Alan Strachan, 'The Irish in Coventry: the Social Geography of a Relict Community', *Irish Geography*, vol. 22, no. 2, 1989.

Alan Strachan, 'Post-war Migration and Settlement in England & Wales 1951-1981', *Geographical Society of Ireland Special Publications 6*, 1991.

Enda Delaney, 'Almost a Class of Helots in an Alien Land: The British State and Irish Immigration, 1921-45', in Donald MacRaild (ed.), *The Great Famine and Beyond*, 2002.

8
Séan Duffy (ed.), *The Atlas of Irish History*, 2000.

9
P. J. Drudy, 'Migration between Ireland and Britain since Independence', in P.J. Drudy (ed.), *Irish Studies 5: Ireland and Britain Since 1922*, 1986.

Ireland has a long history of emigration; however, prior to the 18th century Ireland gained more people than it lost. Influxes of Celts, Christians, Vikings, Anglo-Normans and English settlers had a profound and long lasting effect on the island. In recent centuries, however, emigration from Ireland has overshadowed immigration.[3] Recently, due to the unprecedented economic boom of the 1990s (dubbed the 'Celtic Tiger'), Ireland has increasingly played host to a growing number of immigrant communities, primarily from Poland, Lithuania, Romania and Nigeria.

In the 18th century, Irish emigrants made colonial North America their destination. These were predominantly, but by no means exclusively, relatively affluent Presbyterians from the province of Ulster. Their 19th century descendants applied the term 'Scotch-Irish' to their emigrant forefathers to differentiate and distance themselves from those subsequent impoverished Irish Catholic migrants who fled from Ireland from the 1820s.[4] Although estimates vary, it is thought that during the period 1700-1776 between 250,000 and 400,000 emigrated from Ireland. By the late 18th century, seasonal migration to Newfoundland and Britain was also an established aspect of Irish life and an integral part of the Irish economy.[5] Between 1783 and 1815, following the American Revolution, a further 100,000 departed Ireland for the newly independent United States.[6]

It has been noted that Irish emigration over the last two centuries falls into three main temporal waves.[7] The 'first wave' occurred between 1815 and 1920 with Britain and, to an even greater extent, North America as the main destinations. The Napoleonic Wars (1803-15) between England and France ensured high wartime prices and brought relative prosperity to Irish agriculture; they were followed by a sharp economic depression and an increased outflow of emigrants. Although the Famine years of the 1840s are often viewed as *the* watershed in Irish emigration, by the 1830s large–scale emigration was endemic to all parts of Ireland to an extent unknown anywhere else in Europe; almost 1 million people left Ireland for North America between 1815 and 1845.[8] English towns and cities, which were prospering from the Industrial Revolution, were also increasingly the destination for Irish emigrants. However, the Great Hunger certainly swelled the numbers of emigrants from Ireland and a combination of death and emigration caused the Irish population to plummet from 8.2 million in 1841 to 5.8 million in 1861. North America bore the bulk of the fleeing emigrants; between 1841 and 1860 some 1.7 million Irish had arrived at American seaports and by the time the Irish Free State was established in 1922 a further 2.4 million had joined them.[9]

Tallaghan
Bawn Geesala,
County Mayo:
By the following
year, every man
in this picture
had emigrated.
(1957)

From the 1930s, England became the destination of choice for a 'second wave' of Irish emigrants. The Great Depression of the 1930s and the introduction of immigration quotas greatly reduced the numbers of Irish migrating to the United States; furthermore, disruptions to transatlantic travel during the war curbed emigration to the US and elsewhere.[10] Increased labour demands throughout the war years and in the post-war re-building of Britain resulted in a surge of emigration from Ireland. As the result of a number of factors, the 1950s witnessed the greatest mass exodus of Irish emigrants in the 20th century; these factors included mechanisation on farms which reduced the demand for farm labour, the absence of indigenous industrial development particularly in the West of Ireland, and the continued demand for labour in Britain's main industrial

centres. By 1951 there were 716,000 people born in Ireland residing in Britain, peaking at over 950,000 in 1961 [Table 1]. Although the longest established and, until recently, the most numerous ethnic minority in Britain, the Irish have received relatively little attention within British social history or, indeed, the sociology of migration, race and ethnicity. Instead the focus has been on African–Caribbean and Asian immigration at the expense of those of longer standing and greater numbers, but perhaps of less visibility. Emigration from Ireland fell throughout the 1960s and a significant number who had left in the previous decades returned to the country. However, it wasn't until the 1970s that conditions were considered favourable enough to turn the tide of migration for the first time.

10
Tracey Connolly,
'Emigration from Ireland
to Britain During the
Second World War', in
Andy Bielenberg (ed.),
The Irish Diaspora,
2000.

11
Reports of the
Commission of Emigration
& Other Population Problems,
1948-54.

12
Central Statistics Office,
Dublin.

Many countries (including the United States, England, Canada, Australia, New Zealand and Argentina) greatly benefited from the positive contribution made by Irish emigrants. In the 1960s, approximately 200,000 Irishmen were employed in the British construction industry; these men played a central role in the post-war reconstruction of Britain. Irish nurses played an important role in the early years of Britain's National Health Service, and catering in hospitals, hotels and schools relied heavily on Irish labour. However, Irish men and women have not only worked in the tradit-ional sectors of agriculture, construction and catering. They worked in education and entertainment, as entrepreneurs, became political and religious leaders and even Heads of State in their adopted homelands.

Irish emigrants also made an invaluable contribution to the country of their birth during this period. Indeed, income from 'Emigrants' Remittances' was deemed significant enough to merit a special line in the National Income and Expenditure Accounts. In 1960 this amounted to IR£13.3 million and IR£23.8 million in 1970[12]. This money sustained families and, indeed, whole communities in poorer times and helped to improve living standards in Ireland.

Couple at the Leeds Irish Centre. (Circa 1969)

Brass Street, The Bank, Leeds. (Below:1935)

Following this short-lived economic boom of the 1970s, a 'third wave' of emigration (known also as the 'new wave') was witnessed in the 1980s. Ireland's geographical position between the two great labour markets of the world (Britain and North America), coupled with the fact that for many generations at least one, but usually both of these markets have allowed Irish people unrestricted access, has greatly facilitated Irish emigration.[11]

Irish–born Residents in Britain

LEEDS BOROUGH
1931–1981 CENSUS
(TABLE 1)

YEAR	BORN IN IRISH REPUB/ FREE STATE	BORN IN NORTHERN IRELAND	TOTAL
1931	367,424	137,961	505,385
1941	NO CENSUS	NO CENSUS	NO CENSUS
1951	537,709	178,319	716,028
1961	726,121	224,857	950,978
1971	709,235	248,595	957,830
1981	607,428	242,969	850,397

SOURCE:CENSUS OF POPULATION OF ENGLAND & WALES 1931–1981

Map of
County Mayo
Highlighting
main areas
of emigration
to Leeds

Irish Cross
Channel
Passenger
Timetable.
(1955)

Illustrated map
of Leeds.
(Circa 1948)

The Irish in Leeds

Leeds is situated in the Aire Valley of West Yorkshire, east of the Pennines, in north central England. The modern city spans the River Aire, which meanders south-eastwards across the English midlands, eventually finding its way into the North Sea. Leeds lies between one of England's most important manufacturing regions to the west and agricultural regions to the north and east, and is the regional capital of the Yorkshire and Humber region. Leeds is also located approximately mid-way between the capital cities of London and Edinburgh, and between the Irish and North Seas, Merseyside and Humberside. Its population—715,402 in 2001—makes it the second largest Metropolitan District in the United Kingdom.

Irish emigrants have been settling in Britain in significant numbers since the early 19th century. As a result of continued waves of emigration, the Irish constituted the largest ethnic minority in mid–20th century Britain. The history of the Irish in Leeds is a microcosm of this pattern. Leeds had a significant Irish population from the 1820s, which dramatically increased throughout the 1840s but petered out as the 19th century drew to a close. However, a renewed period of Irish migration to Leeds took place from the 1930s and is the foundation of the present day Irish community.

The Early Years

In Yorkshire in the early 18th century, large villages with a domestic woollen trade grew at such a pace that by the mid–19th century they had become sizeable towns and cities. Leeds is a prime example: the population of Leeds Borough stood at 30,309 in 1775, 53,276 in 1801, increasing rapidly to 152,054 in 1841.[13] This increase in population was primarily as a result of rural migration from the Yorkshire Dales; however the 1841 Census recorded just over 5,000 Irish–born persons living in Leeds, constituting 6% of the total population. No doubt many of these Irish immigrants had arrived as navvies on the construction of the Leeds–Liverpool Canal (1770–1816) and the railways (1834–1849), which linked the heartland of industrial Yorkshire with the Irish Sea.[14] Others, perhaps, began as seasonal migrants to the farms around Yorkshire and gradually gravitated towards Leeds attracted by its employment opportunities: in the woollen and textile industries, in engineering and coal mining.

Tab Street, Leeds, showing Mount St Mary's Church and Convent School (1935)

13
C.J. Morgan, 'Demographic change', in D. Fraser (ed.), *A History of Modern Leeds*, 1980.

14
In 1827, the Select Committee on Emigration noted that in any major construction project of roads, canals or drains one 'should not feel in the least surprised to find, that of a hundred men employed in it, ninety were Irish'.
Second Report of the Select Committee on Emigration from the United Kingdom, 1826-27.

Again, others would have been enticed to follow family, friends and neighbours who had gone before them in a process known as 'chain migration'. Many Irish who arrived during the 1820s and 1830s were handloom weavers who, following the domestic decline of rural textiles from the late 18th century, had begun to descend upon Yorkshire and Lancashire; by the 1830s two-thirds of the 900 weavers in the township of Leeds were Irish.[15] A number of these weavers were from County Tipperary, many other immigrants were from the western seaboard counties and their wives and children took up work in the nearby mills.

The working classes resided in clearly defined areas in 19th century Leeds. In 1839, the Statistical Committee of the Town Council estimated that of the total population of 82,120 in the township, 61,212 were of the working class.[16] The North, North East and Kirkgate wards in particular formed the most densely populated working-class area; the middle-classes tended to occupy the healthier and better situated areas in the Mill Hill, West and North West wards.[17] Thus, the division between the classes was reinforced by geographical isolation.

It is estimated that in 1851 and 1861 more than 80% of the Irish resided in three wards, that of the East, the North and the North East.[18] These immigrants predominantly settled in two districts (The Bank and Kirkgate) on the east bank of the River Aire, forming an 'Irish Quarter' or 'Little Ireland'. These areas consisted of an area roughly enclosed by York Road to the north, the River Aire to the south, Ellerby Lane and Devon Street to the east and Vicar Lane to the west. The houses were back-to-backs, separated from their opposing buildings by narrow, ash-covered streets, which were

rarely cleaned by day or lit by night. They had neither gardens nor yards and opened directly onto the street. The area was also characterised by the poor drainage and sanitation; a report by the Town Council in 1839 highlighted the fact that for a hundred dwellings inhabited by more than 450 persons there were but two privies[19]. Moreover, the numerous redbrick chimneys of the mills and factories emitted thick plumes of smoke, which caused an almost permanent fog to engulf the city. This fog blackened the city's buildings and caused untold harm to the inhabitants living in the vicinity of these manufactories, which included most of the township's Irish population.

Rooke's Fold,
back of East Street, The Bank, Leeds.
(1903)

15
Danny & Helen Kennally,
From Roscrea to Leeds:
an emigrant community, in
Tipperary Historical Journal,
1992.

16
Report by the Statistical
Committee of Town Council, 1839,
in J. F. C. Harrison, Early Victorian
Britain, 1832-51,1988.

17
Report by the Statistical
Committee of Town Council, 1839,
in J. F. C. Harrison, Early Victorian
Britain, 1832-51,1988.

18
T. Dillon, 'The Irish in Leeds,
1851-61', The Thoresby
Miscellany, vol.16,1979.

19
Report by the Statistical
Committee of Town Council,
1839.

20
Edwin Chadwick,
Report on the Sanitary
Condition of the Labouring
Population,1842, in David
Newsome, *The Victorian
World Picture*,1997.

21
J. H. Treble,
'O'Connor, O'Connell and the
Attitudes of Irish Immigrants
towards Chartism in the
North of England', in Butt,
J. & I. F. Clarke (eds.),
*The Victorians and Social
Protest: A Symposium*,
1973.

22
Rev. Edward Jackson,
A Pastor's Recollections,
no.5, 1890.

Wrigglesworth Street,
The Bank, Leeds.
(1918)

The Great Hunger: 1840s & 1850s

The mass Famine exodus from Ireland doubled the Irish–born population of Leeds Borough from 5,027 in 1841 to 10,333 in 1861. Of course, if you take into account the second generation Irish this figure would be much higher. Thus it has been estimated that in the 1850s there were as many as 15,000 Irish residing in the in-township of Leeds, which extended a mere three miles by one and a half miles. The bulk of this post-famine colony also resided in the Kirkgate and Bank districts of Leeds. The Bank, in particular, became synonymous in contemporary writings with poverty, disease, crime, rioting, underemployment and unemployment. Working-class conditions in Leeds in the 1840s can, without exaggeration, be described as sub-human a statement which can be supported by Edwin Chadwick, the Secretary to the Poor Law Commissioners and an ardent sanitary reformer, who reported that for every 1,000 children born in the town, 570 died before the age of five.[20] Almost without exception, in towns of rapid economic growth in north central England — Bradford, Leeds, Liverpool and Manchester — the Irish were rooted firmly to the lowest rung of the economic ladder and at the mercy of low wages and under-employment.[21] Thus they relied for subsistence on their fellow working class neighbours, on charity, on the Poor Law and occasionally on petty crime. Reverend Edward Jackson's recollections of 1847 Leeds provide a vivid and horrific first–hand account of the famine– fleeing Irish:

Tall men, with long coats and hats without crowns, and women, wild and haggard, with numbers of unearthly looking children — strange beings that ran alongside of the men and women, and looked at you out of the corner of their eyes, with a sort of half frightened, half–savage expression. The usual low lodging-houses for this class of people were soon more than full, and they extemporized for themselves dwellings such as none but they would have occupied. Why the Poor Law Authorities did not bestir themselves in time, and open proper places for the reception of these wretched exiles, seems now a strange blunder. Being Irish, I suppose they were not legally chargeable to the township. But it was a great mistake and a woeful economy; for the emigrants brought with them not only hunger but death. In a short time the frightful Irish fever (typhus) was epidemic in all the lower parts of the town.[22]

15

Dufton's Court,
off Somerset Street, Leeds.
(Circa 1899–1901)

The Irish community in Leeds had been associated with the spread of disease long before this outbreak of typhus. A cholera epidemic, which swept across England in the early 1830s, appeared in Leeds in 1832; the first report of infection was of a two year old child of Irish migrants living in the Bank. In the following six-month period the disease claimed 600 lives in 2,000 cases, primarily in the East End of Leeds where the majority of Irish were concentrated.[23]

Typhus, or 'Irish Fever' as it was more commonly known, appeared in Leeds in 1847. Typhus spread quickly and easily in over crowded, impoverished conditions such as was the norm in the Bank; the often deadly organism was transmitted from the affected by body lice. The Reverend Jackson, in his letters and memoirs, recalled the situation in the Bank district:

Here, in this district, which was one of especially Irish character, it was simply horrible. Every place above ground, and underground, was crammed with miserable, famished wretches, scarcely looking like human beings. In one cellar we counted thirty–one men, women and children, all lying on the damp, filthy floor, with only a few handfuls of straw under them; while the frightened neighbours, who would not venture inside the pestilential depth, were lowering water in buckets to allay the intolerable thirst lof the miserable people.[24]

There is an abundance of these dire contemporary accounts.[25] Following the gradual cessation of the typhus epidemic, cholera again returned with a vengeance in 1848 to claim 2,000 more lives in Leeds borough. Once more the East End of Leeds bore the brunt of the causalities. These major epidemics provoked hostility from the host community as the Irish were seen as the disseminators of these killer diseases.

23
Steven Burt & Kevin Grady,
The Illustrated History of Leeds,
2002.

24
Rev. Edward Jackson,
A Pastor's Recollections,
no. 5, 1890.

25
See for example Robert
Baker's *Report on the
Condition of the Residences
of the Labouring Classes in
the Town of Leeds* in 1842
& Frederick Engels'
*The Condition of the Working
Class in England: From
Personal Observation and
Authentic Sources*, in which he
speaks of the impoverished
conditions of the Irish in Leeds
in the mid–nineteenth century.

Corpus Christi
Procession,
Leeds.
(Circa 1920)

Irish-born population of Leeds
LEEDS BOROUGH, 1841–1921 CENSUS (TABLE 2)

YEAR	IRISH–BORN POPULATION OF LEEDS	TOTAL POPULATION OF LEEDS	IRISH–BORN AS % OF TOTAL
1841	5027	152,054	3.3 %
1851	8446	172,270	4.9 %
1861	10333	207,165	5.0 %
1871	10128	256,212	4.0 %
1881	9541	309,119	3.1 %
1891	7166	367,505	2.0 %
1901	6443	428,968	1.5 %
1911	4739	454,155	1.0 %
1921	4027	458,232	0.9 %

SOURCE CENSUS OF POPULATION OF ENGLAND & WALES 1841-1921

End of an Era

By 1880, Irish immigration into Leeds had slowed and by the close of the century had virtually ceased, thus ending the 'first wave' of Irish immigration into the town. It would appear, however, that their situation had little improved; the *1881 Census of England & Wales* highlighted the fact that there was a disproportionate number of Irish relying on the town's workhouse for survival. They were still, for the most part, residing in the worst districts, and to add to their miseries there is evidence to suggest that they had to contend with social and religious prejudices.

The Irish in Leeds: 20th Century

The Irish-born population of Leeds, and indeed Britain, continued to decline in the opening decades of the 20th century; North America was still the primary destination for Irish emigrants. By 1931 the Irish-born population of Leeds had fallen to 3,968, its lowest figure for a century. In truth, there was little to entice Irish migrants to the city at this time; the textile industry was in decline and unemployment was high (21% in 1931). However, seasonal migrants continued to make the annual trip from rural Ireland to the large farms around Yorkshire, Lincolnshire and Lancashire. The 1930s witnessed the beginning of a renewed period of Irish influx into the city. It began as a trickle in the 1930s and '40s but was in full flow by the 1950s.

The 1951 Census revealed that there were 6,218 Irish–born residing in Leeds, an increase of 2,250 persons in the previous two decades, and the population of Leeds Borough for the first time broke the half–million mark. The ethnic mix of Leeds was further added to during the 1950s and 1960s as large numbers of people from the West Indies and the Indian sub-continent arrived in the city. They, for the most part, settled in the inner city wards where rent was cheapest and conditions were worst. Much of this Irish population came to reside in the streets in and around the Chapeltown, Sheepscar and Harehills districts, to the north-east of the city centre. Economically, Leeds was notably prosperous in the 1950s, 1960s and 1970s. As a result of this economic boom, the Leeds Irish-born population surged by another 2,500 persons during the 1950s, a further 1,500 in the 1960s, and by 4,300 in the 1970s, peaking at 14,623 in 1981. This surge resulted in greater needs for the Leeds Irish community:

The Fenton Pub, Woodhouse Lane, Leeds, circa 1940.
(left)

The Regent, Sheepscar, Leeds, circa 1970.
(right)

The Regent,
Sheepscar, Leeds,
circa 1970. (left)

The Shamrock,
Leeds, circa 1970.
(above)

better sports and social facilities were requi-
red and also a Social Services department to
provide advice to new arrivals on housing
and employment. Plans for a purpose–built
Irish Centre were revealed in the late 1960s;
the proposal made provisions for a licensed
club premises, a dance-hall, sports fields and
other social facilities. The Leeds Irish Centre
was officially opened in the summer of 1970,
replacing the older Irish National Club off
Lower Briggate.

  In terms of population, the Census
of 1971 recorded 33,310 people residing
in the City of Leeds born outside of Great
Britain, of which 10,295 were born on the
island of Ireland. In addition to this figure,
one could imagine that there were many
more second and even third generation Irish
(although precise figures are lacking) who
were conscious of and reflected their Irish
cultural background.

Between 1930 and 1980, around one million people emigrated from the Republic of Ireland, the vast majority relocating to Britain; it is estimated that since 1900 two out of every three Irish emigrants made Britain their destination.[26] Why did so many people leave Ireland? Well, in truth, there is no straight-forward answer. The reports of a Commission on Emigration published in the 1950s identified economic reasons as the root cause of Irish emigration. Employment opportunities were poor in Ireland whereas in Britain there was a seemingly insatiable demand for labour on construction sites, on the massive civil engineering projects and in factories in the decades after the war. However, the report added that in the majority of cases the decision to leave Ireland could not be regarded as belonging to any one motive but to the inter-play of several motives — social, political, cultural and psychological. Evidence also attests to the fact that, generally speaking, males and females were motivated by different factors: males more so by a lack of regular employment or a wish to earn better money and females more so by a wish to be self-reliant and independent.

Harehills, Leeds.
(Circa 1972)

26
Liam Ryan, 'Irish Emigration to Britain since World War II', in Kearney, Richard (ed.), *Ireland: The Emigrant Nursery and the World Economy*, 1990.

27
Table 3: In 1961 a post-enumeration survey was carried out for the first time in order to examine census information gathered during the census (see Census 1961, England and Wales, Birthplace and Nationality Tables). On the subject of Irish birth-place the survey concluded that:

A number of persons gave the reply 'Ireland' or 'Éire' with no indication whether this referred to Northern Ireland or the Irish Republic. The people appear in certain tables in the group 'Ireland (part not stated)'. The post enumeration survey indicated that practically all these persons were actually born in the Irish Republic.

In consideration of this 1961 finding, the figures shown in this table for 'Ireland (part not stated)' have been added to those of the 'Irish Republic'.

Irish-born population of Leeds
LEEDS BOROUGH
1931–1981 CENSUS
(TABLE 3)

YEAR	BORN IN IRISH REPUB /FREE STATE [27]	BORN IN NORTHERN IRELAND	TOTAL
1931	3,244	724	3,968
1941	NO CENSUS	NO CENSUS	NO CENSUS
1951	4,788	1,430	6,218
1961	6,632	2,082	8,714
1971	7,580	2,715	10,295
1981	11,093	3,530	14,623
SOURCE: CENSUS OF POPULATION OF ENGLAND & WALES 1931–1981			

So why did so many Irish choose Leeds to be their adopted home? Leeds was notably prosperous in the 1950s, '60s and early '70s with a remarkably low unemployment level at less than 1% in the boom years of 1955, 1961 and 1965 (levels that can be greatly contrasted to the 21% of 1931).[28] This is despite the fact that the city's manufacturing base was in gradual decline from the 1920s to the 1970s; this decline was offset by the rise of an array of service industries. Most Irish men and women were attracted to Leeds by the availability and variety of work. The 1970s construction of the M1 and M62 motorways, at a time when the use of canals and railway had faded, further provided Irish labourers with seemingly never-ending work and reinforced Leeds' importance as a commercial centre, the crossroads of the north-south and east-west highways.

From the late 1940s to the 1970s, the Irish population was most heavily concentrated on and around York Road and in the Burmantofts, Chapeltown, Harehills and Sheepscar districts and particularly around Chapeltown Road, Roundhay Road and Harehills Lane. Other significant Irish clusters were to be found to the north-west of the city in Headingley and south of the River Aire in Beeston and Hunslet, particularly around Dewsbury Road. As the Irish community prospered, many began to move out of the inner-city areas and into more improved residential areas. Generally speaking, since the 1970s the Irish have moved out of the Harehills and Chapeltown areas, being replaced by other more recent immigrant groups, particularly African-Caribbean and Asian. Of course, there were those who remained behind; in 1981 Harehills remained the ward with the greatest

28
David Thornton, *Leeds: The Story of a City*, 2002.

St. Patrick's Amateur Boxing Club, Burmantofts, Leeds. (1972)

The Regent, Sheepscar, Leeds. (Circa 1970)

St. Patrick's Social Club, Burmantofts, Leeds. (1972)

Harehills, Leeds. (1970)

concentration of Irish, followed by the adjoining wards of Chapel Allerton and Burmantofts.

Where exactly did the Irish in Leeds come from? Every county in Ireland was affected by emigration; however, the Western Seaboard counties of Cork, Mayo, Donegal, Kerry and Galway are over-represented in emigration statistics for the period 1926–51. Indeed, the whole of West Yorkshire is recognised as having special connections with the Western Seaboard of Ireland and in particular 'is distinguished by the large numbers from County Mayo'.[29]

In 1990 the Metropolitan District of Calderdale in West Yorkshire was officially twinned with County Mayo. Although Irish migrants from every county in Ireland could be found in any British urban centre, certain towns and cities became associated with particular Irish counties. For example, Leeds is strongly associated with emigrants from Mayo and Donegal (but particularly the former), Huddersfield with emigrants from the *Gaeltacht* regions (Gaelic speaking districts) of Connemara and Kerry, and Sheffield and Coventry with Galway.

29
Jim Moran, 'Goodbye and Good Riddance', Yorkshire Post, 2 April 1990.

22

First Communion, Harehills, Leeds. (Circa 1976)

County Mayo

Mayo is located in the province of Connacht on the west coast of Ireland. The name Mayo derives from the Gaelic *Maigh Eo* meaning 'Plain of the Yew Trees'. It is the third largest county in Ireland (after counties Cork and Galway) with an area of 5,398 sq.km. (2,084 square miles) and a population of 117,446, according to the 2004 census. Castlebar is the county town and also the largest town with a population of just 10,287 (2002); Ballina is the second largest town with a population of 9,478 (2002). Traditionally

Mayo has been one of the least developed counties in Ireland and it has paid a heavy price for underdevelopment in terms of losing entire communities to emigration. A little investigation reveals that the bulk of Irish migrants in Leeds were from the towns, villages and townlands of North and East Mayo—Aghamore, Attymass, Ballina, Ballycastle, Bangor, Belmullet, Bonniconlon, Charlestown, Crossmolina, Foxford, Glenamoy, Killkelly, Killala, Kiltimagh, Lacken, Lahardaun, Straide and Swinford.

Photo Album:
Lough Conn, County Mayo. (left)
Harehills, Leeds. (right)
(Circa 1969)

The Myth of Return

Until the 1960s, the occasion of migrating to the United States was marked with an all night gathering of family and friends which took place on the eve of the departure. This was called the 'Living Wake' or the 'American Wake' and was so-called because it was often the last time the emigrant would be seen in their native land. This was not the case for those emigrating from Ireland to England. Most emigrants left with the view of staying and working in England for a few years before eventually returning home. This is a common feature of migration; for example in his study of Pakistanis in Britain, Muhammad Anwar concluded that Pakistanis left with the intention of returning home with enough money to buy property, build better houses and raise their social status.[30] The Reports of the Commission on Emigration observed of Irish emigrants that, 'in many cases, the out-going traveller was not, in any sense, a permanent emigrant and frequently came and went like a seasonal migrant'.[31] However, regardless of intent the vast majority of Irish emigrants did not return to settle in Ireland and for every returned emigrant there are a hundred who died in England, their fate to die in a foreign land and to be buried amongst strangers. It would seem that there was always a reason not to make the move home. Many emigrants left Ireland with the hope of eventually returning home to settle, but often familial commitments meant that the return was postponed. Although in the 1970s Ireland's economic climate was such that permanent return was a feasible option for migrants, the

24

First Communion,
Harehills, Leeds.
(Circa 1971)

30
Muhammad Anwar,
The Myth of Return:
Pakistanis in Britain,
1979.

31
Reports of the Commission
of Emigration and Other
Population Problems,
1948-54.

1980s were characterised above all by high rates of unemployment and emigration. The phenomenal economic boom witnessed in Ireland from the mid–1990s has at the same time made the country both attractive and inaccessible for many would–be returning migrants. Escalating property prices can mean that only those who were shrewd with their earnings could afford to return. Due to the fact that many emigrants saw their move to England as being non-permanent they consequently never fully settled into English society. One could argue that many were working towards the provision of an ideal life back in Ireland. People are only too aware of the stories of those who returned to find themselves as 'blow-ins' in their own home place or those who, for a variety of reasons, couldn't settle.

Conclusion

Leeds has witnessed almost two centuries of continuous Irish settlement, during which time the Irish have contributed to the economic, social, cultural and religious fabric of the city. In the twentieth century, the 1950s to the 1970s were perhaps the hey–day of the Irish community in Leeds when there was a constant stream of Irish pouring into the city and a vibrant social and cultural scene flourished.

   In 1981 there were 14,623 Irish–born persons living in Leeds; by 1999 this figure had fallen sharply to 9,181 Irish–born persons, of whom 63% were 18–64 years of age and 15% were over 65 years. Without further immigration into the city to augment the existing Irish community it is difficult to foresee its long–term future, and in the current Irish economic climate it is unlikely that Leeds will see the numbers of Irish immigrants it witnessed in the midtwentieth century. At present it would appear that the Irish in Leeds are more organised in terms of social and cultural clubs, and health and housing organisa- tions, than at any time in their history, reflecting the confidence and hard work of the city's Irish community. However, with the Irish–born population of the city in decline, it remains to be seen to what extent the second and third generation Irish in Leeds retain their Irish identity and how they will express their cultural heritage.

Brendan McGowan

Brendan McGowan
holds an MA in Irish Heritage Studies from the Galway/ Mayo Institute of Technology, Galway. This introduction is in part based on research undertaken for his MA thesis entitled *The Irish in Leeds, 1931-81: Aspects of Emigration*. He is currently employed in the Education Department of the National Museum of Ireland–Country Life, Turlough, Co. Mayo. His grandparents Martin & Ellen Ferguson (Co. Mayo) & Conal and Bridget McGowan (Co. Donegal) migrated to Leeds.

Róisín Bán:
Corinne Silva

Townlands:
Leeds and Mayo

Castlebar, County Mayo

Doolough Valley, County Mayo

Oakwood, Leeds

The Pointer Inn, Sheepscar, Leeds

Delicious Dishes Irish café, Harehills, Leeds

Leeds United's Elland Road football ground, Beeston, Leeds

Women's Under 14's Gaelic football, Knockmore, County Mayo

34

M621, Leeds

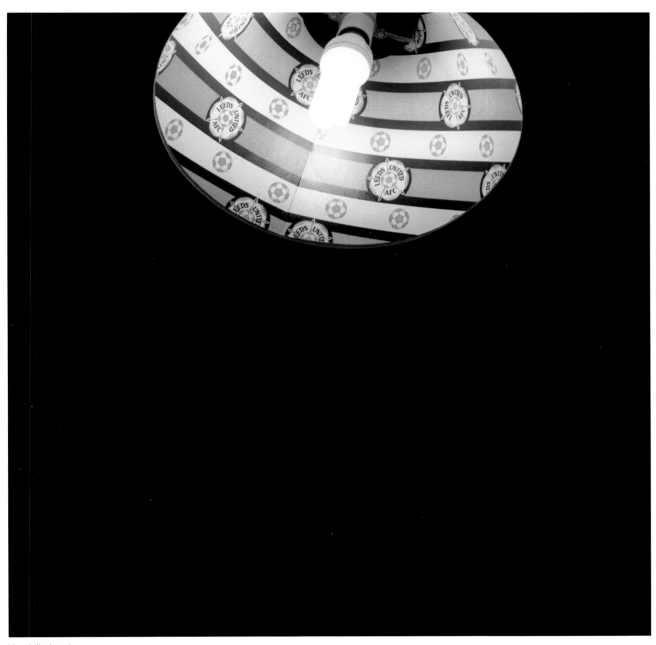

Harehills, Leeds

Harehills, Leeds

M62 Eastbound, Manchester to Leeds

38

Knock Shrine, County Mayo

St. Augustine's Church, Harehills, Leeds

Killingbeck Cemetery, Leeds

Mone Brothers Quarry, Bramhope, Leeds

Sheepscar, Leeds

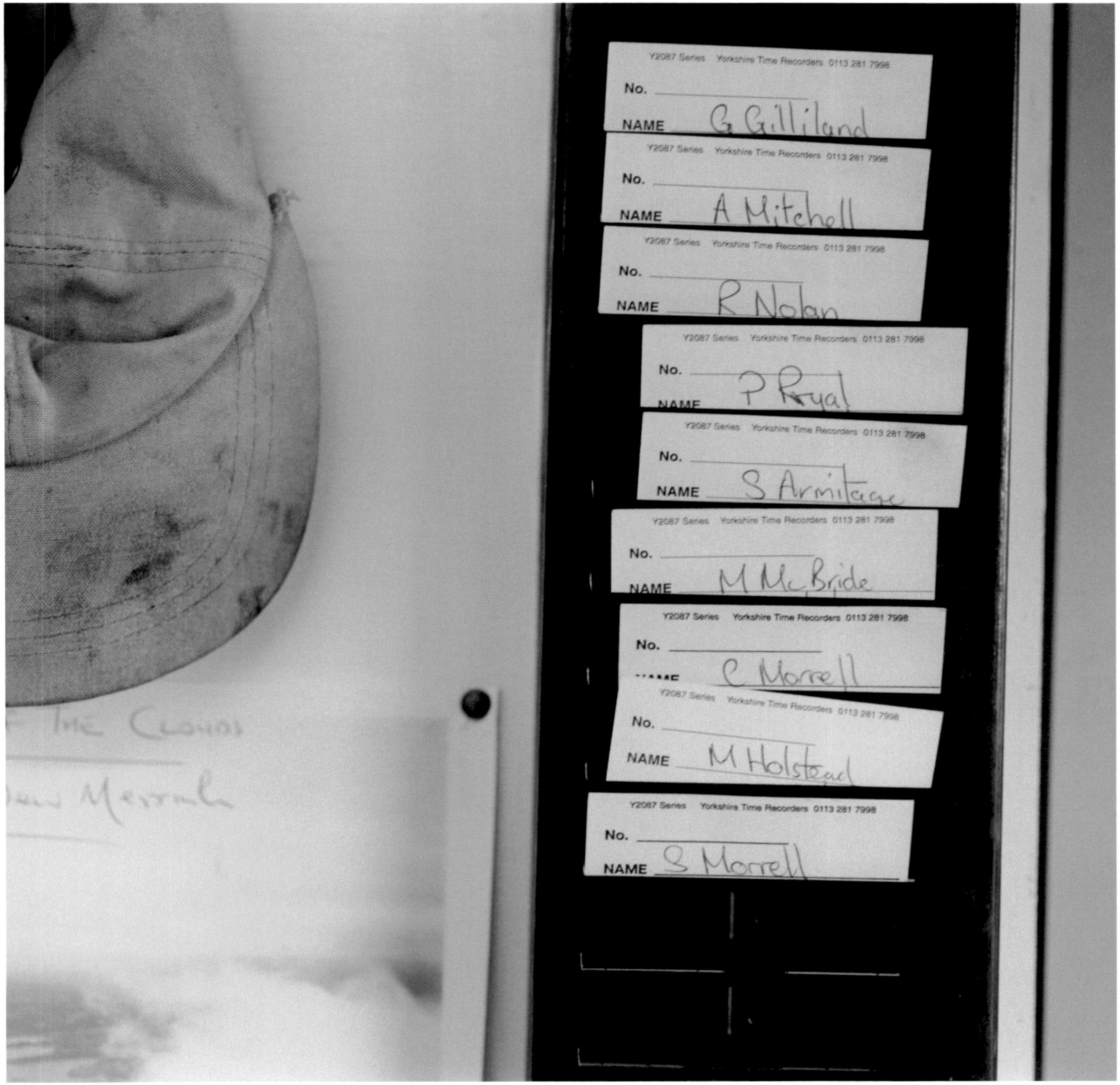

The Clouds

...... Merrah

No.	G Gilliland
NAME	

Mone Brothers Quarry, Bramhope, Leeds

Leeds Ladies Irish Golfing Society, Roundhay, Leeds

Allotment, Burley, Leeds

Train journey from Foxford, County Mayo to Dublin

Train journey from Foxford, County Mayo to Dublin

Knock Airport, County Mayo

Beeston, Leeds

50

Armley, Leeds

Beeston, Leeds

52

Harehills, Leeds

Sheepscar, Leeds

The Skyrack, Headingley, Leeds

Sheepscar, Leeds

Easter Vigil, St. Augustine's Church, Harehills, Leeds

Oakwood, Leeds

Armley, Leeds

Knockmore, County Mayo

Crossmolina, County Mayo

Yorkshire v Mayo Boxing Finals, Leeds Irish Centre

Yorkshire v Mayo Boxing Finals, Leeds Irish Centre

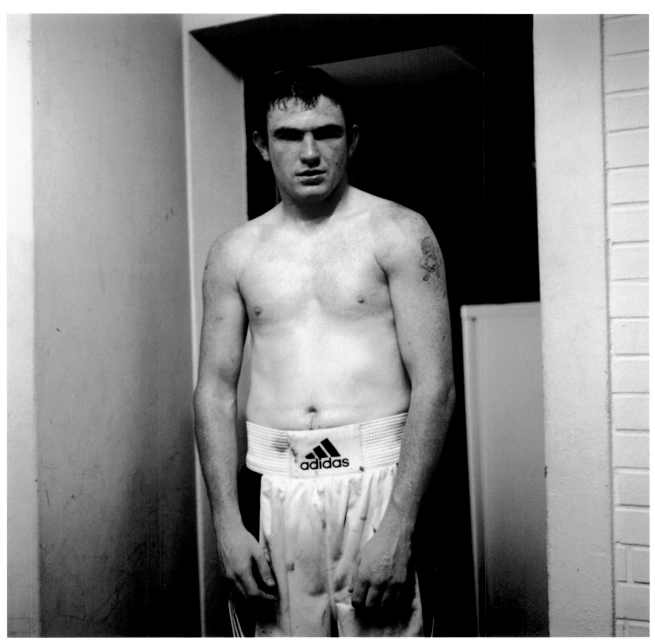

Yorkshire v Mayo Boxing Finals, Leeds Irish Centre

Yorkshire GAA Senior Championships, Beeston, Leeds

Senior Midwife at St James's Hospital, Leeds

Sheepscar, Leeds

Delaney's bar, Harehills, Leeds

Doherty's bar, Ballina, County Mayo

The Old Royal Oak, Leeds

Delaney's bar, Harehills, Leeds

Croagh Patrick, County Mayo

74

Summit of Croagh Patrick, County Mayo

St. Patrick's Chapel, Croagh Patrick, County Mayo

Priest with workmen, St. Patrick's Chapel, County Mayo

Yorkshire rose, Croagh Patrick, County Mayo

Leeds pilgrim, Croagh Patrick, County Mayo

Portraits

Leeds and Mayo

Attymass, County Mayo

Garrett

Anthony

Grace

Sheila

James

John with his children Declan, Finnan and Ciarán

Annie

Laura

Gradi

Kevin

Sean

Sisters Kathleen, Bridie and Nora

Gertie

Declan

Bernard

Born in 1916 in County Roscommon, Bernard emigrated first alone, then a second time with his family, before returning to Ireland permanently. A poet and writer, he now lives in County Mayo.

You had to go somewhere
The times were bad in Ireland. When I went in 1937, Ireland was very down at the time because it got its Independence in 1922, and the period between that and 1937, it hadn't built up, so there was no employment in Ireland. You had to go somewhere else to get a job. I went to Leeds.

Grafting
The first thing I did when I got to Leeds was farming. I worked on a farm for a while and then I moved from farming to public works, building, mostly the building trade. It was all Irishmen working in the building trade at the time. Or most of them. And as time went on I moved into different things. I got into the printing works eventually, before I left England, moved on from there and then came back to Ireland. I was a postman here in Ireland for years before I went to England.

I wanted to do it for Ireland
The war was coming up and I didn't want to be part of it. It wasn't my war and I didn't want to be part of it. And that was the most reason, because they were conscripting people, taking them in. And I wasn't going to become a conscript and I didn't want to become a soldier, because if I had something to do I wanted to do it for Ireland, not for any other country, that was my belief. And when you got back here, they had the army here and I joined the local defense forces here in Ireland instead. And remained here until the war was over and for years afterwards you know.

The Labour Exchange of Leeds
My brother Joe was the landlord of the Regent for years. He had the Roscoe, the Regent, different pubs, you know? The Roscoe, when I got there, was the main pub for Irish. It was a great pub, a grand pub because there was always music and you met everybody from home.

Everybody knew everybody else going into the Roscoe, a great place for meeting. They called it the Labour Exchange of Leeds because if a lad came over from Ireland, he'd go to the Roscoe and they were able to get him a job. There were people there who were contractors, whatever. So that's where they went to for a job when they went to England from this part of the country. They went to the Roscoe.

They were kinda lost, a lot of Irish people. When I say they got lost, you had no proper home, you know what I mean? You were staying in digs, and they moved from one digs to another like.

Stranger in the midst
I get a bit lost in families. Families grow up. You meet them today and you meet them then in six months and they don't look the same at all. You don't know who they are. I'm a stranger myself in the midst. But that's how it is. People change, and they dress different and they do up different and they're not the same and you meet them again and they might have a different colour hair by then than they did the last time.

The Deserted Townland

I have poems stuck around. You'll have
to wait 'til I have a look for them. That's
'The Townland' now, that's one of mine.
I'll read that one for you.

The setting sun its shadows cast,
Where laughter once had been,
Once pipers played, an' children strayed
Old folk their dead did keen.

Where tall trees did grow, an' peasants slaved,
And church bells called to pray,
The simple folk, the nation's cream
At the end of an Irish day.

The piper's dead, the children fled,
No dead, or folk to keen,
All, all's gone, their ghosts linger on,
The fields, they still are green.

If the stranger spoiled, an' the peasant toiled,
Though hard his lot had been,
Why? A townland dead, when the stranger's fled,
And the flag, it now was green.

True patriots dead, then greed it led,
A noble race the stranger's way;
Hate still runs high, men still they die,
At the end of an Irish day.

In music strong, in poem and song
Will the hand of greed decay
Then a dead townland from its grave will rise,
At the end of an Irish day.

32 counties

To me it's all Ireland, because Ireland was
32 counties before it was partitioned. Partition
led to all the trouble and killing, it led to all
that. But to me, my country that I was born
into was 32 counties. It was partitioned in
1922 and I was six years old then. When I'm
writing the poem you might not understand
like, but I'm just saying with our so-called
freedom it means they were still dying at the
end of that time, at the close of an Irish day.

If you partition any country you're
asking for trouble. I often had discussions
with Englishmen now, and discussions,
not arguments, over a drink about Ireland
and Partition. And I'd say to them, "Would
you like it if Yorkshire was divided?"

A load of propaganda

What you're reading now, and what your
parents and people before you were reading
about Ireland, are two different stories
altogether. You're getting a bit of the truth
now. But the people who came before you or
before you were born, they didn't get it at all.
You were getting pictures in the Sunday
papers, and stories, and you were into a load
of bunkum. A load of propaganda. If the truth
was told all the time there'd be no trouble in
the world. It's because of lies and
misinformation that there's trouble. You see,
if you studied it carefully, if people knew the
facts, there'd be no trouble. If the facts were
given to the British people over there about
Northern Ireland, it wouldn't have lasted.
There wouldn't have been as many people
killed as there were. I know that.

I never said I was right. But you came to
interview me and I'm giving you the facts that
I believe. It would be the same if the Prime
Minister of England was there sitting, I would
tell him the same thing.

Helen

Helen was born in 1960 in Leeds of Mayo parents. She works as a French teacher in a local Catholic school and is active in the Leeds traditional Irish music scene.

Shouting my name

At the age of ten I started entering competitions, but they didn't really mean much to me. Now, looking back, I feel they were important but I didn't at the time. I can remember us driving off to London, a big bus-load of us. I think we left about 5 o'clock in the morning, went off to Alexandra Palace in London, and mine was the first competition, and they were shouting my name as I walked in this big room. No idea, ten year old, they suddenly rushed me onto this stool, literally they nearly carried me onto the stool, plonked my accordion on, I played my tunes, and that was the first time I'd won an important competition. It was the All Britain. Of course, the adults, my parents, John who was teaching me, all saw it as a really big thing. It went over my head, a bit too young.

The bug

That was the bug. I played for years. Played in competitions, played in duets with my sister. We won a lot of duet competitions in Ireland, played in trios, and then eventually in the early '70s, John and Maureen, his wife, started a junior céili band. And that's when it really took off, when I got playing with a band, loved it. And I played with Michael and Des, Brendan on the button box, my cousin Huey was on the drums, another cousin Margaret was on the piano, another family, a Leeds family, they played fiddles and flutes. The céili band, we put our hearts and souls into that, and we practised, we must have practised twice a week. And I think in 1973 we did win the All Ireland. It was a real achievement because not many bands from Britain used to win the All Ireland.

Just busy

I played seriously until I was nearly eighteen, and then I moved away, left Leeds, went to do my teacher training in Liverpool. Initially brought my piano accordion with me, then probably lost a bit of interest because I was more interested in student life then, and I can remember a summer holiday, my dad picking me up and sending my piano accordion home because I was afraid it would get pinched. I stopped playing for about fourteen years. Never touched the piano accordion for about fourteen years. Because then I started teaching, got married, had my children, just busy. So the music eventually just went further and further away. And then, perhaps at Christmas would I bring the accordion out, and I'd forgotten an awful lot, and then just didn't have the skills. I never dared join in the music scene because people expected me to be as good as when I was in my teens and I just wasn't. Fortunately, I've got a musical daughter who was learning the flute at school, likes the Irish music, and I used to take her to lessons, and sort of thought, 'Oh, well, I can remember some of these tunes.' So I started practising at home again. Then I'd go up Tuesday nights and started joining in the music again. It's probably taken over my whole life again. And I play all the time now.

Nerves

When I was very young, I had no nerves.
I didn't understand the seriousness of it.
I put hours and hours of practice in, I really
did, but the winning wasn't a big thing to me.
And I've since spoken to my mum's friends
who told me that my mum used to be at the
competitions and, apparently, she was a
nervous wreck. I didn't know this. We were
totally unaware. Apparently, she wouldn't
speak until the competition was over.
And when my daughter then competed
I was just the same. I was far more nervous
watching my daughter compete than
I ever was for myself.

Christmas do's

You laugh now. I laugh because we've always
had big Christmas do's at home, like when
my mum and dad's family were all around, and
they'd be telling these tales, and we'd be not
bored, but thinking, 'They're off again.' And
we're doing it now. We're that age now and
doing the same thing, and you know now why
they took such pleasure out of it when they
got together. The Christmas do's that we have
now, we'll sit around, we'll play our music,
we'll laugh, we'll joke. Our children join in
more now, but when they were little they'd
be dying to go off and watch the telly. When
we were young we used to go to my mum's
family in Barnsley. The highlight of the day
was watching Top of the Pops, not listening
to mum and dad telling stories.

Brendan

Born in Leeds in 1976, Brendan's family returned to live in Ireland when he was three. He still lives in County Mayo.

You can talk to people who came over and slept in the gutter for ten years and then someone who's become a multi–millionaire and retired to the outskirts of Leeds. But you know, the Irish in Britain all have completely different experiences.

Island people

A Kerry priest said to me in Leeds, "At the end of the day, you've got to remember that we're island people, with all the positive and negative characteristics of island people. As islanders, in some ways we're very open and welcoming and in others we're a very closed community. We don't like people coming in and infiltrating. We've still got that sort of mentality."

White labour

I don't know if you know this, but the British government put a block on the amount of people coming in from, maybe, the West Indies and other countries, but not on the Irish. They didn't put a block on the Irish. They didn't put any restrictions. Okay, you needed to have an identity card or something like that, but they put no restrictions because they needed the labour, and white labour was what they wanted. So they weren't doing it out of the goodness of their hearts, or out of our long term relationship.

"All you paddies over here"

I remember my grandfather—he was a quiet man my dad's father—apparently said he was down working somewhere and he got abuse in a pub one night. He was a very mild-mannered Donegal man so it wasn't like him to open his mouth, but this man said, "All you paddies over here," and he turned to him and said, "You wouldn't be able to shit but for us. We're after putting in all your sewerage systems and pipes into the city, and without us you wouldn't be able to shit."

Irish bars have become trendy and that, but you go into them and they're no more Irish than anywhere else. Just because you've green paint and a picture of W.B. Yeats behind the counter doesn't mean it's an Irish bar.

Light years behind

My own father went to school 'til he was twelve here, and it must have been particularly hard for him because the schooling was all in Irish here. So, if you can imagine that you learned English, obviously Irish, your maths was done through Irish, you did Irish history and Irish geography, you know, and then he was put into school in England for two years. So he was light years behind, he was never going to catch up. He didn't know anything about the geography of Britain, he knew the geography of Ireland and his local area, he didn't know anything about the history of Britain. And the funny thing is, our whole history from when you get involved with the British from 1169, our history almost all evolves around Ireland and England and the relation between them. But when you were doing history in England, Ireland only plays a small role for them.

Driving force

My grandfather must have been a businessman in his own head, in his own way, but I've a funny feeling my grandmother was a driving force behind him as well. You don't see these jumps anymore, but my grandfather went from being potato picker, laboured on farms, got into labouring, you know, building labouring, started some construction firm and eventually got into the pub business. Got a big pub, was able to come back, could buy his own home and never have to work again from the late '70s. I couldn't make that jump in life.

Bog tea

If you have a big enough family, where you have a gang of kids, you'd be able to cut the bog for virtually no labour, because yourself'd be bagging it. You'd probably get it machine-cut, but outside that you'd be bringing it home and you'd be saving it yourself, so it's not going to cost you as much. I think if you've been doing it for twenty years, I'm sure it's hard to get out of the habit. It was a social occasion, as well. So you were getting to meet people, and if everybody was out and the weather was good, and I don't know if you've ever had bog tea, but there's nothing better than a bog tea: a cup of tea and a ham sandwich after a hard day's work on the bog.

Part of your Irish tradition

I'm still very much a Catholic, but it's not only that but the girl I'm going out with at the moment she's Church of Ireland, she's Protestant. We've never discussed marriage or anything on the lines of it, but there'd be no such thing as me changing religion, that'd be out of the question. It'd be understood that she'd have to change to Catholicism. It'd be shameful to let that go, it's part of your Irish tradition which would be handed on from your parents as well. So as much as it's religion and spiritual, it's part of your heritage as well.

Michael

Michael was born in Leeds and returned to live in his parents' birthplace in County Mayo as a young child. In his twenties he returned to study for an M.Sc. at Leeds University.

The question of to what extent you retain your accent or take on the accent of your surroundings is very much a personal choice, I believe. My Uncle Joe, he's lived in Leeds for forty-three years, and if you hear him he sounds just like any other Crossmolina man. He's great like. Hasn't taken on any hint of a Yorkshire accent at all.

Put on a nice white shirt

A typical person that you get up in the Irish Centre is a guy in his 50s, late 50s, early 60s maybe, who's spent his whole life over here, done alright, probably got kids, grandchildren here. I was just looking round at them yesterday, and I thought, 'You can't say that the Irish look very much like the English, that there's not much difference between them.' There is just a look that is Irish like, and I was looking at these guys at the Irish Centre yesterday, and that look is kinda… they dress up a little bit to go to the Irish Centre because it's Sunday afternoon or whatever, but they put on a nice white shirt, and it always is a white shirt you know, open to about here and lovely and clean, and a pair of slacks, and they might have a chain with a cross on it, and they have like steely grey hair, receding a little bit, nicely brushed, a weather-beaten kinda face, a bit red, maybe a bit of sun at this time of year and a silver or gold watch, a bit of a paunch like.

Mum, she's not really religious, but part of being an immigrant is you almost over-identify with the things that make you different.

A classic tale

Mum left Leeds in '79, left her family, her brother and sister behind. Jimmy died, I guess in the very early '90s. That's her brother. A few people have said that he was a real character. He'd a real quirky, whacky sense of humour, a bit mad in the head. He died at fifty years which was very young really. He never married, and from what I can gather talking to different people, I think it was basically drink that was the approximate cause of him dying. I think the story is that he just came back from the pub one night, turned on his gas heater and forgot to light it or something because he was drunk, and the fumes just killed him. It was quite sad, it was a couple of days before he was found and stuff, because he lived on his own. To me that's just a classic tale of a poor Irish immigrant. It would have been good if he'd been married, just to have somebody.

103

Bridget

Bridget was born in County Mayo in 1934. She retired as a District Nursing Sister in Leeds in 1995. Now, much of her time is spent volunteering for the Simon Community.

The family rosary

My father was a Pioneer all his life and my mother liked sherry at Christmas and times like that, but she wasn't a drinking person. The family rosary was said at night and in the morning. Before we went to school we always blessed ourselves and said our prayers to the guardian angel on the way out, so we were covered for the day.

"Don't ever refuse anybody food"

Once when I was scrubbing the floor a tinker came to the door and they wanted some milk and I was, you know, out of the door and the dresser was over there where all the milk was, and I thought, 'I can't walk across this floor.' But my grandfather came in and he said, "What does she want?" and I said, "She wants some milk." And he said, "Well, give her some." So I did, because he said. Well, I was seventeen and a half when I came to England so I might have been fourteen or thirteen or something then, and he said, "Don't ever refuse anybody food." And I always remember that.

I remember my grandfather, you know, going through the fields and he'd have his rosary beads there saying the rosary and we were children like ducks after him. I don't know what we were collecting, going out for the cows or something, bringing them in to milk.

Well, my younger sister went to the convent school. The rest of us went to the technical school. It was, I think, ten shillings a year to go to the technical school and it was £10 in 1952 to go to the convent, so most of us went to the technical school. Three of us nurses and the rest worked in offices.

Arriving

I travelled with other people that were leaving home. We parted company at Holyhead, I think, and then I went on to London. And there was somebody on the boat and he was from Galway, I don't know who he was, I never saw him since, but he came with me to the hospital. The Sister introduced me then to some Irish girls and I felt at home immediately. I never felt strange or anything. And then one of the nurses took me to the Labour Exchange or somewhere to get cards and a ration book, because things were rationed then as well. Because I was brought up in the country sweets didn't come into it, except very rarely, but it never bothered me. But the fact that we had coupons to buy chocolate, I thought this was wonderful!

104

Bridget

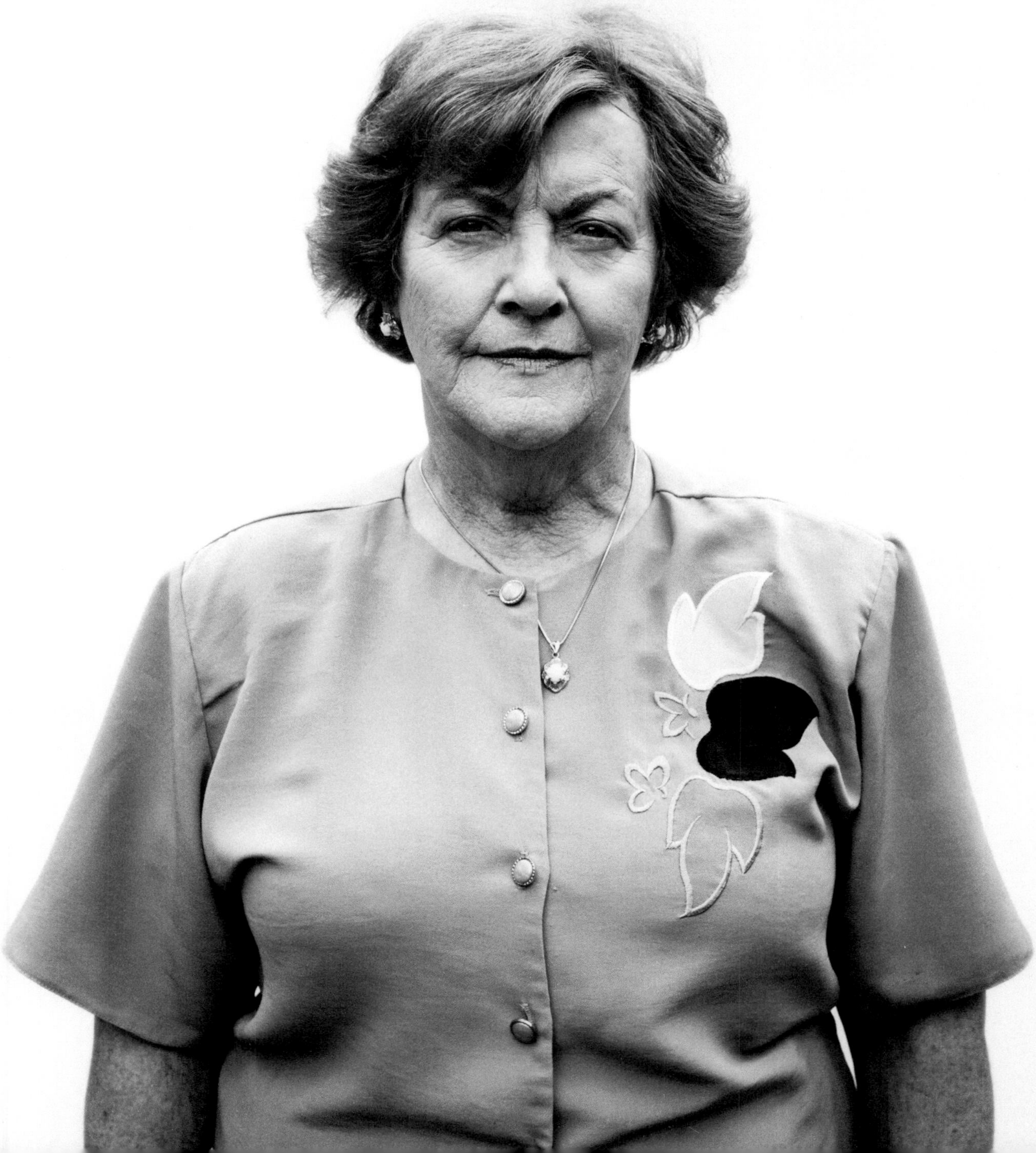

Treated like royalty

I came to St. Andrew's Hospital in London and, you know, being brought up on a farm, I was the second eldest of nine, and because I was healthy, you know, work wasn't a problem to me. And to have one and a half days off a week where you did nothing only please yourself, to me it was a very easy life. And people used to say, "It must be hard being on the wards all day long," and I never thought it was hard you know. I thought it was a life of luxury and we had our own bedroom, we had clean linen every week and cleaners cleaned the bedrooms. We were treated like royalty as student nurses really. Our salary was £6.18.4d a month, but then we were fed and we had our uniform and everything, so really it was a lovely life. In my third year I used to send £2 home every month. And then when I qualified I put it up to £5 a month, because as a staff nurse you got £14 a month then. Most of the nurses sent money home. I couldn't have trained in Ireland, because to train in Ireland in 1952 you had to pay for your training and buy your uniform and we hadn't that kind of money. And as well as that, when we came to England we were given our passage as well, I don't know, was it £10 or something? So, you know, we have a lot to be thankful for. Well, I certainly have.

I know my son said once, "You don't mind what we do," and I didn't as long as they were happy, and so he didn't work at school. But I used to think, 'I don't mind if they end up sweeping the floor, or cleaning the town hall steps, you know, but I'd like them to have a degree first and then they can scrub the floor.'

Dermot

Born in Leeds in 1964, Dermot returned to live in County Mayo with his family when he was ten. Apart from working intermittently around Europe, he has remained there ever since.

A shadow

I hated going back to Leeds. Every summer my mother sent us home here for the three months to my grandfather who lived down the road here. My grandfather, he was a man of the land; he sowed all his own crops by hand, he cut his own hay by hand. And I was always with him, I was a shadow.

A cruel thing

At the end, when the school holidays were over, one day I was in the middle of the country, swimming in the lakes, and next thing I woke up in Leeds, and I used to rebel big time to it. It was a cruel thing to do. And then in '74, I came home from school one day and my father said, "Right, come on, get ready, we're going," and I said, "Where?" "We're going back to Ireland to build a house." That was it. I thought I'd won the lottery. My father built the house and I was here with him. And we were here ever since.

I haven't gone back to England much. I get a cold feeling down my back when I see Leeds. I just love Ireland, I love the country so much. I have to be in the countryside, I have to be in open places.

Europe

The old-fashioned way of knowing who your neighbour was has gone. The original sort of unity of the village has broken up. A lot of people are coming back but they're finding it very hard to build here now because of all the restrictions from Europe: where you can build and who can build and how you can build and what kind of house you can build. It's really tightened up. European culture, it's doing away with identity. What's going to be next is the national flag. They have a European flag anyway. I like the fact that we have a strong Irish identity and it's a very strong identity throughout the world, no matter what country you go to. Even in any backwater you'll walk into a Paddy. It doesn't matter where you go. But I think we're losing our identity.

Going round on donkeys

They still think we're living in cottages, thatched cottages, and still going round on donkeys. It's an awful cultural shock for people coming back after fifty years. If they've lived in England for fifty years, it's a big cultural shock.

In all the small villages, like my village, you always had a pub, and you had a church and a school, and you always had a small shop. And all the small shops are gone now. You're forced to go into the big towns, to the multi-nationalist stores. In the small villages, you'd got that community little shop where everyone met. You always met there on a Friday for your pension or family allowance and everyone knew each other. They were half of them related anyway, those that came in. It's all gone now, because they'll all go to Dunnes and Tesco.

Careful who you insult

You have to be awful careful. We're still
working a clan system. It's all very clannish
round here. We're all related, big time,
everyone's related to everyone. All different
families just branched off, but you still have
a connection. So you have to be awful careful
who you insult. You can insult the whole
village you know.

Break your gun

I don't really start hunting until November
when the frost comes in and then we go
across the fields walking with the dogs, like
you see on television in England. That's
when we do the hunting, the proper hunting.
Pheasant, woodcock, ducks, snipe. For the
table. We eat everything we shoot. It's not just
shooting them, it's eating them. It's a lovely
delicacy, it really is a delicacy. We don't shoot
everything though. We shoot to a bag, there's
a limit of four birds, and once you get to
four birds you break your gun and that's it.
And after that then you're just walking the
dogs. But it's just the pleasure of being out
there. Fantastic like! You cannot beat it!

Eddie

Eddie was born in 1945 in County Down.
He has lived in England since 1966.

One of the things that people who live in England, born and brought up here, do not understand is the psyche, if you like, of an immigrant.

You were different

I was born in the North of Ireland which is under British rule, but nevertheless everything is so different there to what you find here: the language, the way you speak, the mode of speech, the speed at which you speak, your accent, all of those things made it very apparent that you were different and you didn't belong here.

Back to your roots

Someone will make comments to you which will make you very conscious and aware that you don't belong here, that you weren't born here, you're not one of them as it were. So I think most immigrants go through that identity crisis and so you start to question what you're doing, and question your own identity, if you like. And there's two ways you can go, you can try to assimilate more, try to adopt the accent and all of those things. A lot of people try and do that because that takes away the pain, but they only end up looking ridiculous. Fortunately, I took the other route which is to go back to your roots, and look at your identity in terms of your nationality, and then you go back to the literature and the music and all that.

I've been in the company of white men in hospital, you know when I worked in hospitals for the Health Service, who would tell racist jokes and would make comments about black people, purely on the grounds that because I was white I would be happy to join in with that, you know, and were quite taken aback when I would object to it.

Even in my own land

I was born in a small village. We were one of only a couple of Catholic families in the village, and the kids that I played with, there were about four or five lads my age in the village at the same time and they were all Protestants. And for two weeks during the 12th of July things they wouldn't come out and play with me. So I was on my own. Even in my own land, in my own village where I was born, I recognized that I was different, somehow.

A poor substitute

I do resent and I do regret the fact that I had to leave my native home in order to be independent. It does anger me that I was not allowed to be Irish in my own land. So there's an element of that in it that I find painful, if you like. And I have this life-long desire to go back there to live and spend my days, even though the substitute for that is I've put in my will that I want my ashes taken back there and scattered. So I rely on one of my children to do that. But that is a poor substitute for living in your own land.

109

Economics

It was economics, basically. I was an economic migrant. During the '60s, and it always has been, the North of Ireland was financially a mill-stone around the neck of the British people, even though they were never told that, they never had that explained. For example, during the '60s there was a whole range of shirt factories and garment or textile industries that were encouraged to go there by the tax concessions that the government gave them. And all they did was employ women, because women were able to be paid much less wages than men. There was generations of men in places like Derry and Belfast who never, ever worked. The grandfather, the father and the son would all grow up and never have a job. The women all worked and the men raised the family, basically. Plus the fact that they had a streamlining system in the education system. They say, "You're no use, you're gonna be working as a labourer," or whatever, "You can go on the dole or you can emigrate. You can go into the Civil Service or get a reasonable job," and so on. That's how the system operated and I was one of those who was streamlined into the 'no use 'channel, if you like. So it was pretty obvious to me by the time I was a teenager that I wasn't going to go anywhere.

Beg, borrow and steal

People who came to England and then would come back for a holiday, they always came back well-dressed even if they had to beg borrow or steal a suit. They always looked as if they were well-off and they would always talk as if they were well-off, and the kids in the village would say, "Oh, Mick's doing very well in England, that's my ticket out of here." A guy would come home from America with a big American car. I didn't know at that time that you could buy an American car for next to bugger all.

One of the up-beat things about coming to places like Britain is that, for all its faults, it's quite an open society and you have a lot of freedom, and you've escaped the constraints that a small close-knit community has on you.

Norah

Born in Yorkshire in 1944 of Mayo parents, Norah emigrated to County Mayo with her Irish husband in 1972, where they built a house and brought up their children.

Black and white

I think there was a lot of racism among the Irish in Leeds to tell you the truth, about the blacks, coloured people. They would have felt that they were of a lesser status. Maybe it was thought that white was superior. That's all Irish people were short of when they went to England or America was the black skin.

History repeats itself

Now what annoys me is when I hear people here. Some of these people probably never left or never had to leave. Mind you, I don't miss an opportunity to say it to them. But they get annoyed now when they see people coming in here from other European countries. I think, maybe, a lot of it is because of the colour of their skin. Now I know that maybe there are some people who are using the system and milking the system. They're exploiting it. But I don't think they're any different to how the rest of the world is, you know. Whether you're English or Irish, I think there'll be people within your ethnic group who will be willing to exploit the system, rip other people off. I think there are an awful lot of decent people who are coming here for a variety of reasons, probably to look for a better way of life than what they're leaving, whether it's in Africa or Eastern Europe. They're only looking for a better way of life, and yet it annoys me when people say we shouldn't be letting them in. Because millions of people left here and went to America or to England, and I'm not saying that they had an easy ride when they got there, I don't think they did. I'd say a lot of them had a very tough time. I know that my mother and father would remember the times when they would have seen notices up, 'No Irish Need Apply', whether that was for jobs or for accommodation. And, I suppose, for human beings history repeats itself, doesn't it?

111

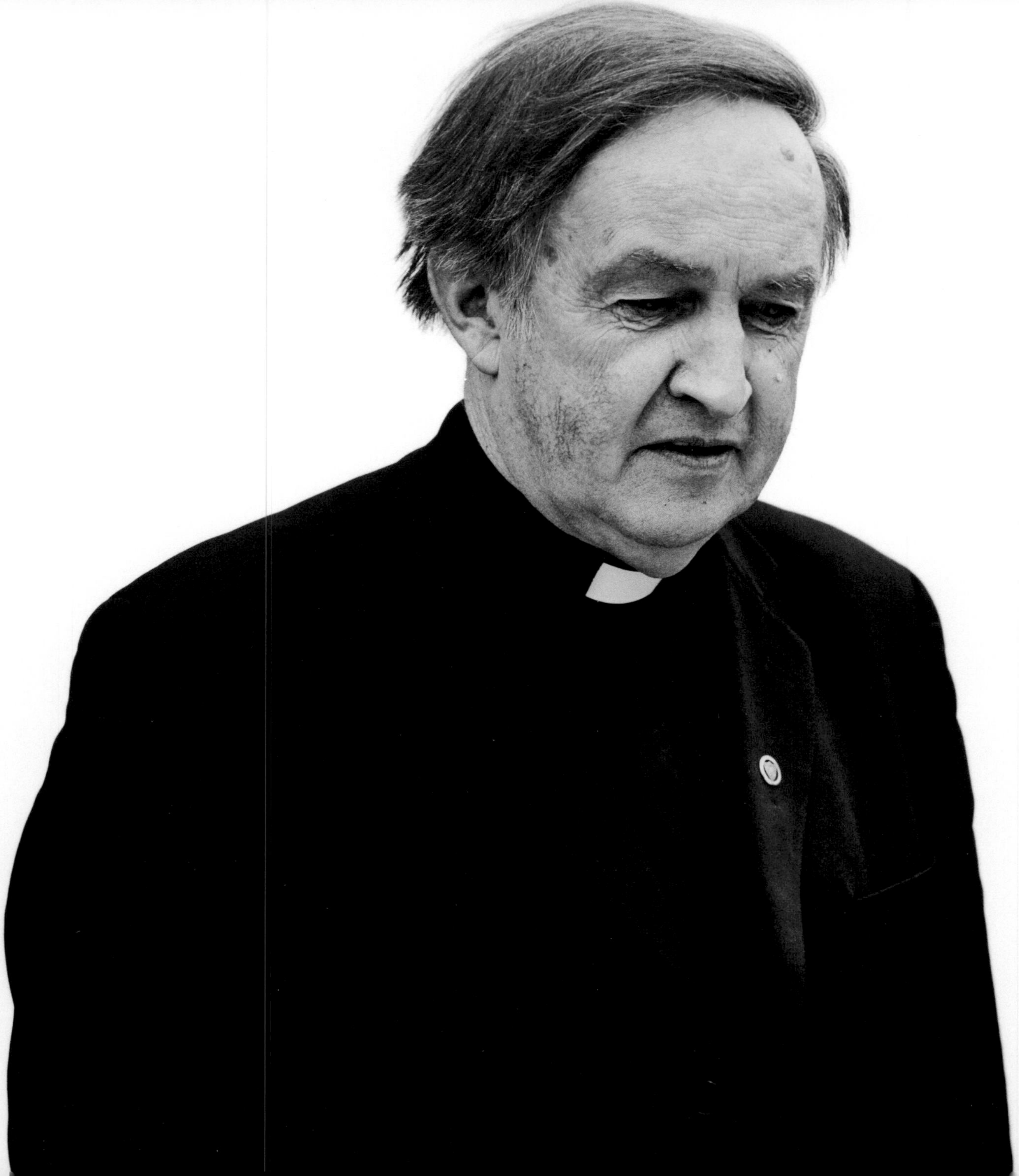

Father Martin

Father Martin was born in County Galway
and came to Leeds diocese in 1968.
He has been based at a number of parishes
in Yorkshire and his current post is at the
Immaculate Heart in Moortown, Leeds.

Culture shock

It was a culture shock coming from rural
West of Ireland to a mining community.
But the people were quite friendly there, and
there were some Irish working in the mines.
At that time in Ireland there was a surplus of
priests, so the general trend for a lot of people
was to move out and be challenged. There
wasn't that much of a challenge in Ireland in
those days, in the '60s.

Becoming a priest

Well, you don't decide. You try. You just go to
the seminary and you just discover whether
it's for you or not. A lot of people in those days
started but didn't finish. Some people of their
own volition wouldn't finish, they decided
that this wasn't for them. A lot of people
would be told that it wasn't for them. If you
didn't pass exams and one thing and another,
you'd just be told to go, really. Which wasn't
very nice. That was part of seminary life early
on. You'd be down at breakfast and you'd
discover maybe that the person beside you
wasn't there this particular morning, that he
was gone to the train.

You have to deal with people as you find
them, and that's a big difference coming from
an academic background in the seminary to
dealing with people. Because in those days in
the seminary it was very academic orientated,
and then when you come face to face with
people in a waiting room you might have all
the answers in theory, in a book, but when
you deal with people it's a different ball game
entirely you know.

We were very shielded in the seminary, kind
of immune from life itself. I haven't had any
bad experiences really. I came to a very
supportive environment in comparison to the
individual who would come looking for work
on his own. Everything was provided for me:
house, food, house-keeper, in those days.
They're not so plentiful nowadays, but they
were in those days.

More Irish than the Irish

It's mostly second generation Irish now
because, since the '80s, there has been very
little immigration. So, you don't meet that
many young Irish people, direct Irish people
with Irish accents, shall we say, but you
do find that some of the second generation
are more Irish than the Irish themselves.
For example, during World Cup situations
when Ireland were doing well, and you
still see people going along with Irish jerseys
and so on. On St. Patrick's Day in a primary
school, you had children with shamrocks and
harps and one thing and another.

Well, it's good for people to be proud
of their heritage. We were always taught
in the seminary not to be ashamed of your
accent or anything like that, but obviously we
were taught to be able to speak clearly so that
people would understand. I would maybe
retire at home. But having spent thirty-six and
a half years here now, you're more attuned
to the Church in this country than you would
be in Ireland you know.

Irene

Born in County Kildare in 1955, taxi driver Irene came to stay with her sister in Leeds when she was seventeen and never left.

Big bands

Coming from a village to suddenly a city, it was like, it was fantastic for me because I'd never experienced that side of it before. And obviously one of the main things for me, daft as it sounds, was, you know, the weekends and that, when we actually used to go to the Irish Centre.

We'd be there three nights: Friday, Saturday and Sunday. A great environment, meeting up with the people from back home. It's daft, you kind of come all this way and the first place you actually head for is to be with the Irish community, and at that stage they had a brilliant Irish Centre in Leeds you know. Every weekend it was what we classed as being the big bands, Big Tom, Brendan Shine, you know, and it was great, great atmosphere, great way of life.

Part of something

Years ago, when I came to Leeds, people they were renting and sharing houses. The Irish would all rent together you know. You'd have the little cafés, the little Irish cafés here and there—there might be one in Harehills and one in Beeston or whatever, and at the end of the working day, the blokes who were on their own they'd all head for wherever it was, you know? I think they headed for them because they actually felt part of something. They actually felt as if they were heading for their life there. Their extended family.

'Proddy dog'

I'm actually Church of Ireland, now you see! Surprise, surprise! Everybody thinks that everybody's Catholic in Ireland, daft as it sounds. There was one or two kids I used to play with and they used to say 'proddy dog' and that because they didn't have any friends that were Protestant, but that never bothered me, do you know what I mean? It was never a big issue that I was Protestant, kind of thing.

Change

In the village where I come from it's totally changed. I would go back home and a lot of people, I wouldn't have a clue who they are. I'd never seen them before. Sadly, it'll never go back to the way I remember it, you know? And I loved it as it was and a lot of people I speak to will say the same, "Ireland is not what it was." But I think they have moved on, you know?

Bricks and mortar

To me, my home is Ireland. Always has been and it always will be. I can't ever see a time when I won't class Ireland as home. The fact that I have a house here and that I live here and that I work here is immaterial. To me it's bricks and mortar. My home is Ireland.

Whenever my time is up I would certainly want to be buried in Ireland. That's where I was born and bred, that's the country I really do love and that's, you know, where I would want it to all end for me.

Patrick

Patrick was born in County Down in 1918. He emigrated in 1939, working around Scotland and the north of England before settling permanently in Leeds.

The monopoly

The reason why I left home was because there was no life there. There was no opportunity for people there if you were a Catholic, because they done their best to get rid of all the Catholics to reduce the population there. That was my honest opinion.

They were domineered by the Unionists, I don't like to use the word Protestant. They were Unionists and they had the monopoly of the country. They had the monopoly of everything. You got what was left.

The dole

You certainly had a little bit of homesickness all the time, but you knew there was no future there to go back to. There was only dole, and you may have got a few odd weeks' work here and there and then you were back on the dole. But then when the war came they sent everybody that went near the Labour Exchange over here to work. They didn't send their own Unionist crowd, they found them something because they wanted to hold their population there.

Strangers

I travelled from London to different places, working, wherever we'd get the best money. I was working in Glasgow, just outside Glasgow. I found that the money was a third better down here than in Scotland, so then I decided that I would hang around here. So I moved about Yorkshire here, different places, and even done a lot of open-caste

coal sites. Miners, they didn't like us, but we got used to them and they got used to us. But we realized that mining villages was the same as a very small community, and they didn't like strangers coming in to take away their living. We were digging coal from the top and they were mining. You could understand, but that was the law of the country. We weren't doing any harm, only looking for a living.

"Put wood in t'hoil"

Every place you went you had to adapt yourself to their dialect. I've never had any trouble here, but when I was working at Flockton, out there in the Barnsley area, I was coming into the canteen one day and someone shouts at me, "Put wood in t'hoil." I said, "What in the name of God is he talking about?" I had to go and ask him personally what he meant. But then, you see, I realized it was 'close the door', when he told me.

To your own advantage

You had to be aware of the differences. You had to be aware. It made it easier for you if you did stay around Irish people, but even here in Leeds I had some of the most best friends of English people that you could ever wish to have. And then, when you were working on jobs and everything else you made yourself as sociable as possible for your own good, for your own self. It was to your own advantage. You got on better instead of if you knew everything and big-mouthed and everything else.

Going home

People say, "Are you going home?" but
I'm passed that now and I don't never...there
is no home. There's only my brother's house
and he died there before Christmas. So it gets
scarcer and scarcer every year. There's a lot
of people you see still goes home to Ireland.
They say,"Oh, I've been home this year.
Have you been home? Are you going home?"
I think that's sometimes now a bit unusual,
because I mean, at my age, at eighty-six, past,
there's a lot of thoughts gone out of my mind,
but then... when your old home is gone…

So I went home to my brother's
funeral there before Christmas. I didn't know
a soul. I didn't even know my own nephews.
There were some from London, some from
Birmingham, some from Oldham. I never seen
them. We weren't a family that was very close
to one another. When we come over here we
all went our own way. Fended for ourselves.

Oh, I used to go home when my
parents were alive, for a week or a fortnight.
And this was the fascinating part about it,
when you went over and the first thing when
you were meeting people, they'd say, "When
are you going back? When are you going
back?" That's God's truth now.

I would have loved to have an accordion but
I never could afford to buy one. When I arrived
in Liverpool I had £3.10 in my pocket, and
of course you never had no steady income.
There was a brother in London and there
was another brother at Ellesmere Port, but
I landed in Liverpool, I got a job in Liverpool
but I never bothered them.

Both sides

These B Specials and people there on Easter
Sunday morning, we come out of church with
the Easter lily on. You would get held up and
rifles put in your face, and saying, "Get that
lily out." Because it was green and white.
These little things.

You can't blame one or the other. One
aggravated the other. Frankly, it's a business.
Well, I knew the IRA done some horrible
things, but the other side done horrible things
too. Not this war but the other war previous
to that, there was some awful dirty work
going on. Both sides. And there still is. I put it
out of my mind that you get Paisleyites there.
I don't want to get involved in anything now
because I left it, and I never regretted the day
I left it.

Myself and the family

Religion to me, it's a personal belief, and
leave other people alone. If they want to go
to the pub, if they want to go to the cinema,
if they want to go to church, if they want to
go, I don't bother. Because that's the way
I think about it. Because I always put it down
as a personal belief. Personally, I believe in
myself and the family, as long as they're
alright. But interfere with anybody else, no.
You've gone through life and you've seen it
all yourself. I've seen all sorts.

116

James

Born in Dublin in 1950, the youngest of thirteen, James has lived and worked around Britain since 1972.

I'm the baby out of the family. I was the nuisance out of the family too.

I survived

I pulled into Bolton, outside Manchester, where my sister's mother-in-law lived, and I worked in a cotton mill. For about... the money was... Jesus Christ... I think it was £36 a week. We had to get up at 5 and finish at 3. In them days I didn't feel settled. I was back and forward. I survived. I went back and forward and then I came over here. I survived.

I hadn't a washer

I think it was in the '80s when my Mum died. I was living in Liverpool then. The police came to the door, told me my mother died, and I hadn't a washer, I'd nowt', no money at all. So the police had to ring the eldest brother John to pay for a ticket for me and my girlfriend to go back. I went back. I stayed in Dublin, in my ma's house. I stayed in Dublin for a day. And the brothers and sisters, they were all arguing about this and that, and I said, "I don't want anything at all. Keep it." And me and the Scotch woman, we got back on the boat, and I hadn't a fag, and we came back to Liverpool.

I had the best of jobs in Dublin, me. I worked for Jacob's, the biscuit factory. I worked for Rowntree's. My brothers got me the best of jobs but the drink got in the way again.

Some were good, some were bad

I got a job with an Irish firm, Conlon Finnegans. A good firm to work for. But half the Irish, some were good, some were bad. And then the drink got to me again and I got sacked. I love me old drink. Well, it's better than taking drugs isn't it? Or smashing windows? Or hurting people, isn't it? Then I got a job with a Donegal man. Sometimes he'd pay you, and other times he wouldn't pay you. Then I got a job with... who else did I get a job with? Kavanagh and Manny, I'm sure they were from Galway. And half six in the morning, rain, hail and snow, you used to go round the wagon at the back, and there'd be tools and about ten, twelve bodies in there, and you'd travel about an hour, an hour and a half to get out. Believe me love, it was hard work. But you had to do it, personally speaking, you had to do it to survive. Because if you wouldn't have done it, you'd have been dead.

The Scotch woman

Oh, she liked the drink as well. She didn't help either did she? You've got to laugh. The blind leading the blind, put it that way. She was from Glasgow. Well, me and her fell out. We got a council place, me and her, in a place outside Glasgow. And me and her, I couldn't get on with her family. So I left her. I told her I was going to the shop for some coal and I came back to Manchester.

Doss house

I went then to a place, they called it the
School, a doss house. I went in there, and
it was rough, rough. You had to hold your
own. There was Irish, English, Welsh, Scotch.
And they used to give you a bowl of soup
at night-time, but you had to keep all your
clothes on you, because if you left them
beside the bed, they'd have been took. I was
in the doss house where fleas were a hundred
per cent. I left there. Then I went to Salford,
Manchester, and then the travelling boys
come down, and I done a bit of work with
them, and moved on with them. I had my
own caravan. Some was good, some was bad.
Worked, got up in the morning 5 o'clock, go
for tarmac, go and do whatever we had to do,
and all that, that was it. I got fed up with them.
They moved on, I can't think of the town.
So they pulled in onto York Road, and I said,
"I've had enough." No more tarmaccing,
no more selling three-piece suites. When you
have enough, you have enough, you know.

I do nowt. Just clean me place up, do a bit of
cooking and have a drink. I'm an alcoholic
love, and I've never sold any stuff out of this
house. You have to be hard, not hard, you
have to be cruel to be kind. Do you not think
so yourself?

Joe

A joiner by trade, Joe came to Manchester from County Tipperary and started working on the roads at the age of fifteen. He now runs a popular Irish pub in Leeds.

Should have been eighteen before you had your national insurance card. You had to give a wrong name and a wrong date of birth or whatever at first. And then when you were eighteen you went down and said you'd just come over and you got your own national insurance number. Everybody was doing it so nobody said nothing. It was the accepted thing to do.

The Princess Maud

It could have been England, it could have been America, it could have been Australia. They were the three main parts to go. But England was the handiest, and it was the cheapest passport across. It was the cattle boat that we came on. The boat would dock in Birkenhead first and they'd haul the cattle off, and you could hear all the cattle and you got all the smell of the cattle shit and everything coming straight up. And that's what we had to travel in. That was the way back and forward. It was called the cattle boat, The Princess Maud. Then you came into Liverpool to the docks. And once you got off in Liverpool you just decided which city you were going to go to. You had no plan. You found out where all the Irish lads was drinking and you went to a pub, you mixed in with them, and every Irishman got a start in the pub. Most Irishmen at that time got paid in the pub. So you found out there where all the work was.

You worked

You worked on the pipes, the gas lines, working on putting the cable in. I worked as a joiner. I worked with the farmers for three months of the year, back end of the year. You went for the tattie picking, you went for the beet, you went for the corn, you went for the onion picking. You gave three months for the farmer, living in a shed. There could be five hundred pigs in the shed and there was a little corner screened off where you had to sleep with all them pigs grunting and groaning. You had no water to wash yourself, you had to go out, they called it a river in Ireland, they called it a dyke over here. You went out to the dyke on a frosty morning, at six o'clock in the morning, you washed your face and washed as much as you could. And you never seen town until Saturday night. You went in, you done all your shopping in town, you got drunk, you come back home on the Sunday with enough food to keep you going for the week. You washed all your clothes in the river. And you lived like that for three months. But the money was good. You had no chance of spending it so you could save it up.

When you finished in the evening picking the beet, you put your dinner on. You were straight to bed. You were up at six. On a day like this you'd be up at six and out picking the beet, and it was thick with ice, with the dew, and your poor fingers would be falling off and you'd be clapping your hands.

Spalding in Lincolnshire, that was the worst place. I worked in Spalding in 1958 and there was a pub there called the Hole in the Wall. There was a big brass plaque, about two foot by two foot, and on it, 'No Irish Allowed In Here,' on the door. But one day, 'To hell with it, I'm going in.' I walked in and I got served. They never put me out.

Any woman you want

At Spalding in Lincolnshire, Christ, they were all farmers' daughters. The farmers used to hate us. The locals used to hate us. Because the Irish lads could have the pick of any woman they wanted. Their accent, you see, the Irish accent. You went to town on Friday and Saturday night, all the girls were there. Any woman you wanted to go with you could have went.

Home-from-home

There was so many Irish people over in the '50s and '60s you always felt at home anyway because once you went to an Irish pub, you went to an Irish dance-hall, you always mixed with your own people, so it was like home-from-home in one sense. The loneliest time was when you went back to your room. You had no television, no radio, no carpet on the floor, you had to light the fire, you were freezing for an hour.

Black mariahs

The police was very hard on us when we came over first. You know, outside the Irish dance halls. There'd be always two or three, we used to call them black mariahs outside the dance-hall waiting for us to come out, to see if we'd start staggering, or start falling. Anyway, you were grabbed and put in the van and locked up, which you wouldn't have seen outside any other nationality dance-hall.

A lot of it was brought on by themselves. The way they carried on, going out and getting drunk, wanting a fight. If an Irishman heard that there was a bloke in London that was a hard man, another fighting man, he'd go to London and want to have a go at him to prove that he was better than him. It was a lack of education, that's what it was. It still happens today. Young fit men, they have to get rid of it somewhere you know. Look at all the fighting that's going on now in Leeds. In town, people getting drunk. Young kids is only doing what we did in the '50s and '60s. The cycle is still going you know.

Bring your own shovel

When most of the Irish people came in the '50s, the English government sent over for them, between the '40s and '50s. Sent over for them, and when you came over here, you had to bring your own shovel with you to work for the contractors. You had to bring them over with you on the boat. Can you imagine coming with a shovel on the boat? Christ Almighty. You'd be embarrassed now, wouldn't you?

An Englishman wouldn't get a job on a building site. An Englishman wouldn't work on the cable. He wouldn't work on the gas. That's why the Irishman dominated that type of thing.

Joe

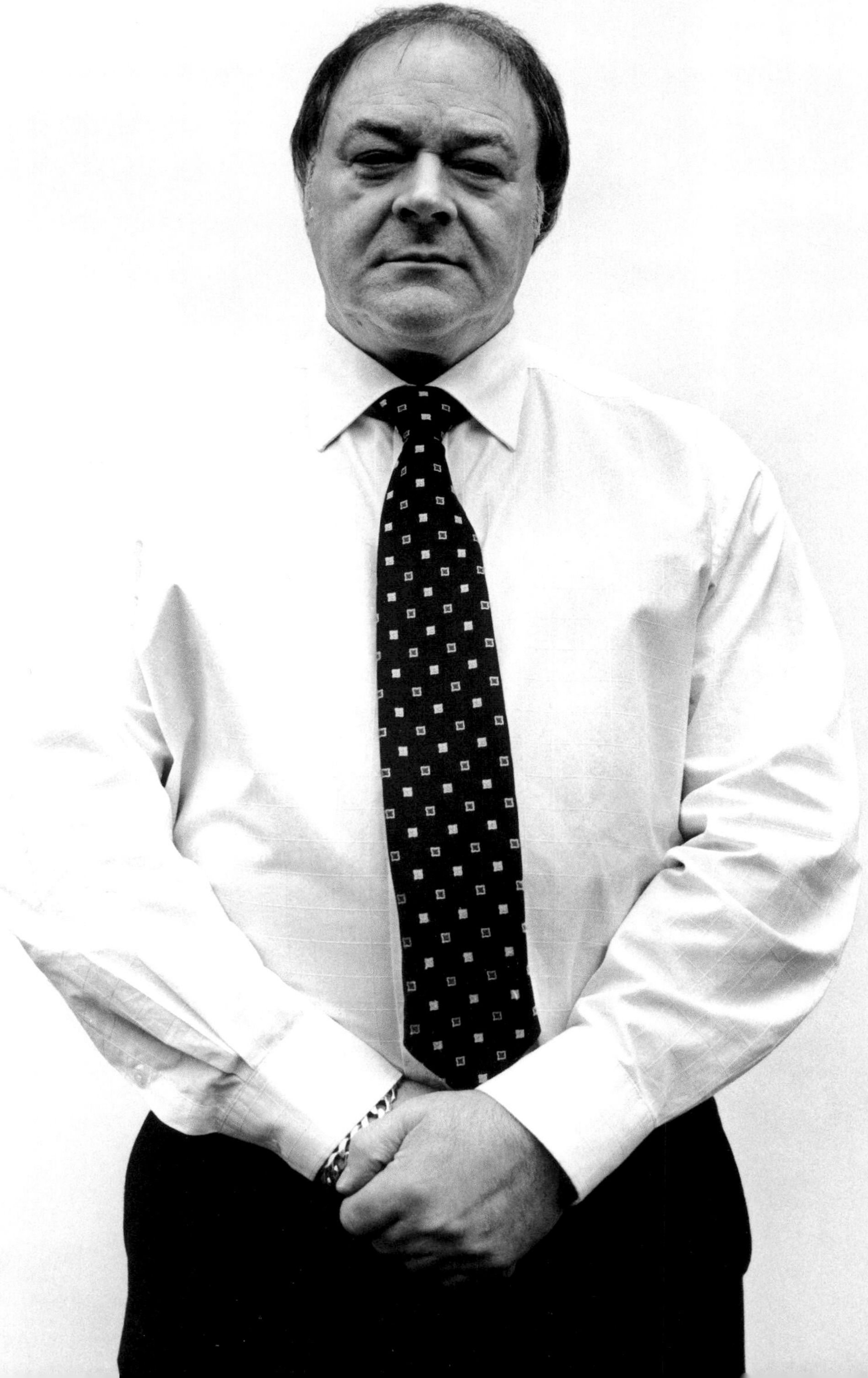

Cable-laying

Ten o'clock in the morning you'd have your breakfast. And there'd be one lad, he'd be called the tea-boy, the chef, and he'd make the breakfast. And he might have eighty half pounds of steak. And you got a loaf of bread, with a pot of tea out of a bucket. And you were sat at the side of the road, eating.

You'd jump in a wagon and you might travel from here to Huddersfield and there'd be no canopy, an open wagon, in the middle of winter. It was pure slavery when you think about it. That's the way it was. You accepted it. And you couldn't rebel against it because you'd just get sacked. It was a way of life and you accepted it.

It was dangerous work. That would never be allowed to happen now. Nobody wore hard hats, no jackets. If you were seen wearing a glove you'd be sacked. If you went out on most of the jobs with a pair of shoes you'd be told, "Go home, you're no good." Because you couldn't dig, you see, with shoes. If you went out with any jewellery on you, you were a nancy boy, you were told to get to hell. You were no good, you couldn't work.

Such a feeling

You know, when you land there in Ireland and you get off the boat or off the plane, you feel different, something comes over you. I can understand when the Pope landed in Ireland, he went down and he kissed the ground. You feel like doing the same thing. Such a feeling comes over you, 'I'm home.' Once you land in this country, you feel so down and depressed for weeks.

Your own language

Now things have changed. There's so many Irish people in business here now: doctors, we've lawyers, we've solicitors, we've judges, we've every type of contact now we didn't have before. We'd nobody really to turn to for advice when we came over. We have now. It's like, now, I will go to an Irish solicitor because I keep the tradition up, because he understands me, what I'm saying. I'll use an Irish bank and if there's an Irish doctor, I'll use an Irish doctor. They talk your own language and it's easy to explain to them.

Jason

Born in Leeds in 1971 of Irish parents, Jason lived and worked in County Mayo for a number of years before returning to Leeds. He is on the committee of, and coaches for, St. Anthony's Gaels Gaelic Football Club.

Brainwashed

We've been brought up with Irish music, listening to the records and tapes. Whenever my mum was in the kitchen she always had the Irish radio on, so we'd always hear the songs all the time. That's probably how I got into music, yes. Just constantly listening to it. Been brainwashed.

Home

For my dad, after his parents died, then this became home, England. That's where his family was. Which is the way I would see it as well. This is home really. Whereas I was brought up thinking Ireland was home. After my dad's parents died he lost that feeling that Ireland was home. He's still very much an Irish man, without a doubt, and very strong Irish culture. But home is where your family is, isn't it?

I was a driving instructor and the Celtic Tiger was really booming in Ireland at the time. I'd just come back from Ireland on holiday and everything was really buzzing over there, there was so much work and everything, and I thought I might as well go over and try it.

A shilling for luck

They used to have little parties when people were leaving, and people would try and give some money to people who were going, like a shilling or something, you know, for luck. I learned from people in Ireland what it was like for them staying there, trying to survive when there wasn't much around them, how grateful they were for the money that was sent back to them from their siblings in other places, and how much they really, really missed them. How sad it was for them to stay there. Not many people appreciate that. They only see their side of it.

Like it or not

Children have more choice these days. Some kids were actually forced to go Gaelic football training whether they liked it or not, same as some were forced to play music whether they liked it or not, forced to go Irish dancing whether they liked it or not, forced to go to church whether they liked it or not. Parents are more sympathetic to what children want these days, more than when I was growing up.

123

Role of the Church

The role of the Irish Church now has changed. Definitely there was a lot of control, like in my dad's time, from the Church. For example, his family had to pay for their seats in the church. There's like, the collection, if you know what I mean. So if you had a big family, and my dad came from thirteen altogether, including parents, that's quite a lot. You had to go to Mass, and if you didn't you'd be the talk of the town. If you done anything wrong, the priest would read your name out in the Mass, things like that. The priests and the teachers were very closely connected, so if you did anything wrong at school, or vice versa, the other one would find out. There's not as much control now from the Church in Ireland. I think that's also the same here. People are more willing to actually think for themselves rather than just believe in what's been told to them. They're not as scared of the Church.

A slap with a shovel

I think quite a lot of Irish people who came over here were quite proud, they might not have liked it, but they just got on with it. They had no other option, there was no point complaining, there was nobody to complain to. If they complained to anybody at work they'd probably get a clout, a slap with a shovel. So they just got on with it.

I'd come back straight away

My dad never talked about how sad he was leaving Ireland or anything. But when I came back for a Christmas holiday just after I'd gone over there, my dad told me that when he got to London the first thing he did was write a letter back to his mum. Because that's what she asked him to do. And he wrote back that he was living in this digs, it was crap or whatever, but he also wrote to her, 'If I had enough money, I'd come back straight away.' So he was telling me that in a way to say, 'Look if you don't like it you can come back.' He never told me that he was not happy when he came here. But he told me then.

Joan

Born in 1931 in County Tipperary, Joan came to England to train as a nurse before working in the USA as a nanny. She later settled in Leeds where she worked for almost thirty years at St James's Hospital and St Gemma's Hospice.

Round here everyone knows me, everyone speaks to me, but not one would ask you inside the door for a cup of coffee. People are frightened to have you inside the door because they don't trust people.

The herring pond

My mother used to call it the 'herring pond that's taken all my children from me.' At that time, going over to England was like going to Australia. You know, the big cattle boats and people being sick everywhere. It wasn't fit for animals. My mother said I cried all night. My father used to cry, and you never saw him crying. That time it was so hard leaving Ireland.

The poverty

It was terrible at that time in Ireland. The poverty was terrible. The poverty was absolutely shocking. We walked four and a half miles to school, and four and a half back. Can you imagine nine miles a day? To go to a convent school. They were very good but they were cruel as well. They were very, very cruel when I look back.

In January—you didn't have running water—we used to go out and the barrel of water that would be underneath the chutes outside, there'd be ice on it. Sometimes you'd be going out to break the ice. It was dreadful. But it's gone the other way now. It's gone too much the other way. Have you been over lately? Beautiful places now. I'm happy for them.

Being lonely

I got the train. And you cried all the way to Dublin in front of everyone. My father, he was a station master, and I used to put my head out of the window, waving a toilet roll from the toilet, until he went out of sight on the platform. Oh it was awful, it was dreadful. That's why a lot of people commit suicide in London you know. A lot of the Irish being lonely. It's nothing to do with the country here. It's to do with your blood, where you were brought up.

In a nutshell

You weren't told about babies. You didn't have a clue. I remember my waters breaking on the street and I didn't know what was happening. I thought, 'I can't be spending a penny, it just feels different.' It hurt me leaving Ireland so ignorant. That's it in a nutshell.

Night duty

I worked fourteen years on night duty. With the kids, I never had to leave them. I used to work at St. James's. At that time we lived in Harehills. We left Harehills, you know, up to the Carr Manors, and then I was still at St. James's working night duty. You got two buses then ran all the way up the hill to get the kids from school. I've never chatted to even my family about the past, they wouldn't want to know. When I look back at that hill, and I think now, people in cars must have thought there's a mad woman here racing up. But you love your family, you didn't suffer at the time.

125

I don't fit in with myself

I got on great, but inside you're very different.
I feel like I'm living under a different identity
here. I fit in with everyone, but I don't fit in
with myself. When I go to Dublin, I don't look
for it, but as soon as I put my foot on the soil
I can feel all that draining away, and I come
back to being the person I was and always
have been. Can you understand? Crazy isn't
it? Because you don't want to feel like that,
but you can't do anything about it.

Leeds Irish Centre

I used to go with my ex-husband and three
other couples and we all sat together.
But then when you get divorced, the other
couples go together in a taxi, so you don't
fit in any more. And then, they're very,
very cliquish because they're going there
for years.

A free life

Sometimes when I feel I can't get going,
I feel all achy. Because I'm pushing myself
over the limits because I'm all alone. And
then I get frightened because I think, 'Is there
something seriously wrong with me?' I feel
I'm aching all over. I don't tell my family
that, though. Because I want them to
have a free life.

John

John was born in 1943 in Belfast where he lived until his early twenties, moving then to Liverpool, Sheffield and finally Leeds.

The family rosary

We weren't a particularly religious family, although my father, he was a Catholic and he believed in it. We were the sort of Catholic family that we'd be late for Mass, we'd stand in the church porch-way during the Mass, we'd disappear once the sermon started. So it was very much going through the motions you know. And then I remember this campaign for the family rosary. My father was very keen on this so we thought we'd all have to say the family rosary together, and this just degenerated into giggling fits; so that didn't last long.

A latent anti-clericalism

I was sent to this Irish Catholic boarding school, so I was out of Belfast for most of the '50s. That's where I spent a lot of my formative years. It was a Catholic school so it was run by priests, and you had to go to Mass every morning. It was quite religious, and quite Irish Nationalist. And I think this was why I developed a certain dislike of the clergy. Most of them were alright, but there was one character who was a religious fanatic, another who was basically a sadist, and there was another one who, you don't realize when you're a kid, but basically, in retrospect, he obviously liked little boys. I don't think he ever did anything but he clearly liked to surround himself with pretty little boys. So I think a latent anti-clericalism developed when I was at school.

Qualitative difference

As you get older you start thinking, and by the time I got to 'A' levels, basically I had big doubts. I didn't really believe everything I was told. When I first went there I was probably quite religious, and from the age of eleven to fourteen I took it all very seriously and I really believed in it. But over the years doubts started to creep in. I could never understand how murder could be a mortal sin, and how impure thoughts and actions, to use the jargon, could be mortal sins as well. There seemed to be a serious qualitative difference between murdering somebody, selling people drugs that might kill them, and doing perfectly natural things and perfectly natural thoughts, and I asked the priest this, and he basically couldn't answer it. He said you shouldn't think about these things, and the wisdom of the church and this sort of carry on. So I said, "Sod you, mate."

The showband generation

I was one of the showband generation. The showbands were fantastic. I can still remember The Royal Showband and the Capital Showband and Joe Dolan and the Drifters. I remember the Ulster Hall in Belfast, a big public hall in Belfast. The only two things that ever seemed to be able to fill the Ulster Hall were either Ian Paisley having one of his bigoted rallies or the Royal Showband on New Year's Eve, playing.

Nice Catholic girls

In the North it was more Catholics than
Protestants would go to the showbands.
Basically if you went to these things you
met Catholic girls. Nice Catholic girls would
only let you go so far. But if you went to
the University, if you went to the Floral
Hall, there were lots of Protestants there,
so young men would go to the more
Protestant dance-halls, because Protestant
girls, although they still had their limits,
would let you go a bit further you see.

The Pioneer Total Abstinence Association

It was this thing, you vowed never to drink
alcohol, and you had this wee badge that
people wore, good Catholics who never
drank alcohol wore. But the big thing was
to acquire one of these badges, and you
wouldn't actually wear it, you'd keep it hidden
behind your lapel, and then you'd try to get
into the dance-hall. You'd pretend you were
sober and you'd put this blooming badge
up so the bouncer would say, "Oh, he's a
Pioneer, we'll let him in."

Change

A memory I've got is going to see the Wolf
Tones in the Leeds Irish Centre. This was
shortly after the hunger strikes and they
played this song about the hunger strikers
and they asked for silence and it was a very,
very emotional experience, and you could
have heard a pin drop. The emotion was
palpable. I heard them again about ten years
later, and they did the same song and they
asked for silence, and of course people at
the bar just kept on yelling. Things have
changed so much.

Since the Good Friday Agreement,
Belfast is booming, big shiny new buildings
all over the place, and it's sad that people
are still squabbling about power sharing,
because economically they have left all that
behind. But given all that, I still wouldn't
want to go back because beneath the
surface there are still currents of the old
tribalism and bigotry.

I was at a party once and somebody
called me 'Paddy' and I wasn't a bit pleased.
I said, "My name's not Paddy, it's John."

Tom

Born in 1944 in County Mayo, Tom first made the journey from Ireland to Leeds when he was eighteen. He worked across the north of England before returning to his place of birth in 1985 with his Cumbrian wife and children.

A better craic in Leeds

I didn't find it all that different in Leeds because half the Irish people from around here was in Leeds at that time. There was a better craic in Leeds than there was here. We mixed in Irish circles like, lived in Irish areas, sort of thing. You didn't really meet much English people. And if you went dancing they were practically all Irish dance-halls around about. The same if you went in to the pub, Irish music and all that sort of thing.

When I left here, I was building a dance-hall here in Pontoon, and we were on about £6 or £7 a week. The first wages I got in England was £24 a week. So there was a big difference. But that was extra hard work now we were doing, you know. The average wage would have been £14 or £15 at that time.

Better than the towns

Murphy's of London. They're still going, you see them with the green vans, there putting in cables, underground cables, electric cables. I stayed there until about June and then we went to Clitheroe in Lancashire. You could go to the farmers there, helping them with the hay like, and you'd live there for however long they took you. They'd hire you for a month, but after a fortnight you could finish if you wanted to and go to the next one. So that was the first introduction I had to meeting English people and English countryside. It was absolutely lovely up there, up where they made that vet's programme, Hawes and North Yorkshire. It suited me better than the towns anyway. Leeds was smoky and dirty at that time.

Neither fish nor flesh

I feel sorry for the Irish fellas in Leeds and them places, the cities, that didn't get married. Living in flats, it's lonely, you know what I mean. Actually, I think it shortens their lives. Sort of been thrown on the scrap heap and living alone, and that sort of thing. I've seen them in cities in England and it's sad like, you know. I suppose you turn to the drink then for company. And even if they came back here they're neither fish nor flesh. Even if they came back here they wouldn't really fit in either, they're too long gone like. And they'd hardly know anybody, like so.

With open arms

Actually the population of Ireland went up for the first time in 120 years, it said yesterday. It's only on four million now, like. That's in the Republic, in the 26 counties, like. It's very sparsely populated. There's a woman from Moldova, she works over at the Pontoon Bridge Hotel. Because the young Irish people won't do that sort of work anymore. If they're coming in to work and do what we did, I think they're good for the country and welcome them with open arms. To go to so much trouble to try and get into a country, they must be suffering where they are, mustn't they, you know what I mean? If all they want to do is work it's a shame to deprive people of it, isn't it, like? A lot of immigrant labour built Britain up. From here a lot of it, like.

Whatever fate has laid out for you

There was three of us supposed to go to England at that time, and then they started this River Moy drainage in Mayo, the biggest project of its kind ever done up to then. So we didn't really have to go to England if we went on there. But one lad went on this Moy drain and stayed at home, and me and the other fella went. So, peculiar, he got killed with a dumper on the Moy just two years after he started there. And the other lad who came with me, John was his name, we moved about together, we moved to Cumbria together, he got killed by the self same sort of a dumper about 1980, I think that it was. There was Sean, John, myself and Paddy, all more or less the one age group. John, he got killed by a dumper, Sean let himself go with the drink and that, and he died in Manchester, and Paddy died in Rotherham of cancer in April 1998. That's three of them gone, and all young men enough, in different ways. It shows you whatever fate has laid out for you, that's what'll become. So I try and keep away from dumpers as much as I can.

Winter

I tell you when we first came over to England it was one of the hardest winters ever recorded, I think. Six weeks of hard frost and you couldn't pour concrete and you couldn't work on construction. With us only being there a few months we weren't prepared for it, you know what I mean. We used to go shifting snow during the day. You get a few bob for that. There was nobody working that winter. It was hard on people. You wouldn't have any money or anything like.

But anyhow, we got through it like. That was my first experience of Leeds, that hard winter, and as far as I was concerned it could be that way every winter. But it was just a one-off. The frost was so deep in the ground that it was busting the water mains and the gas mains and we used to go out repairing them, so it created its own work, sort of thing.

Tom

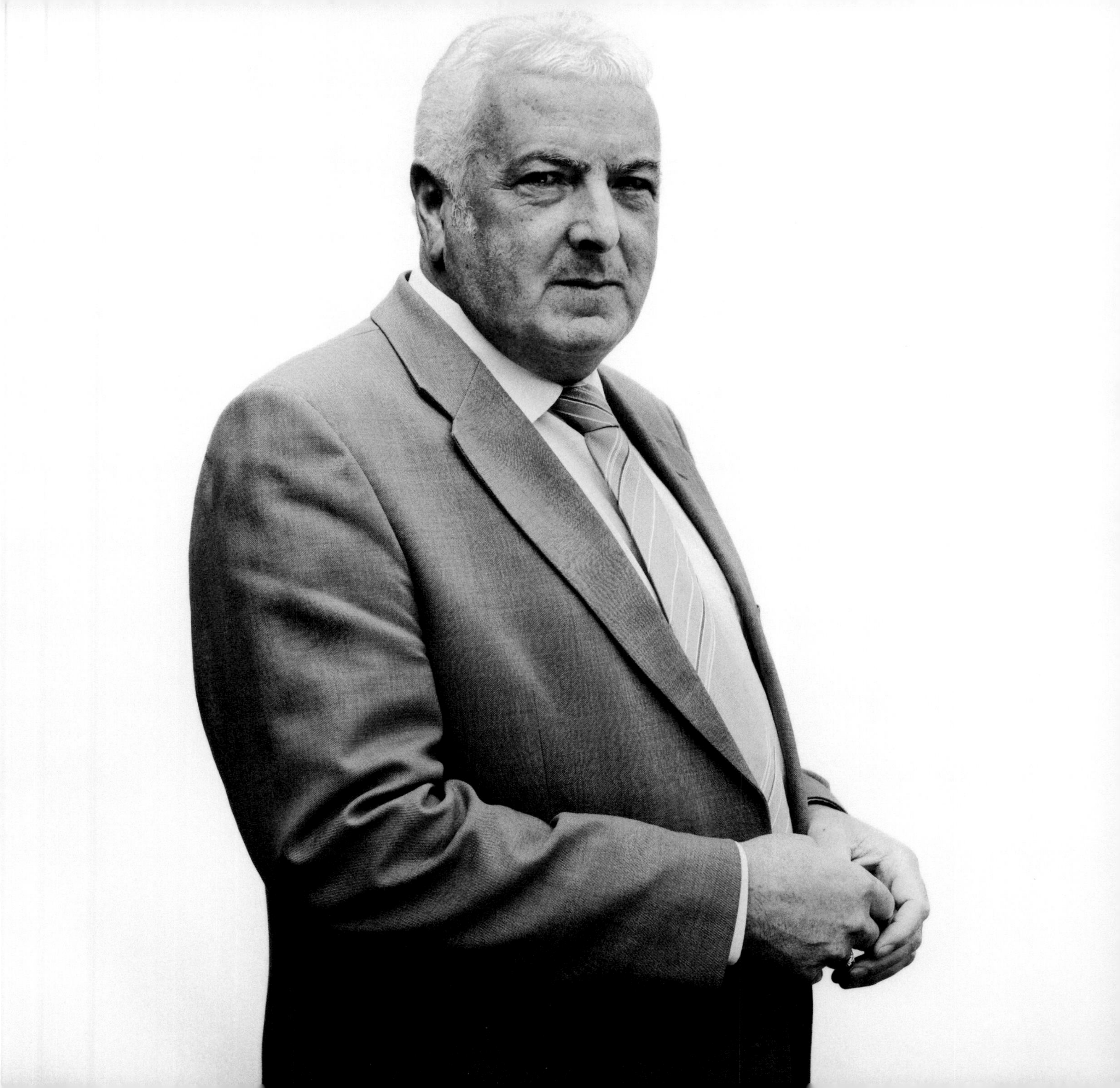

John

John was born in England in 1945. His family returned to his father's birth place in County Kerry soon after he was born. At seventeen John returned to live in England once more, eventually settling in Leeds.

I was born over here in Wolverton, Buckinghamshire. Had the removal van been on time I would have been born in Ireland, but it was six months late, and the family moved over when I was about four months old.

One in four hundred

I went to the Catholic school run by the Christian Brothers. They had a Canon who used to come round and visit us at school and it was a big day when the Canon came. I was the only Protestant in the school. And every time he came, he came and shook me by the hand. So I used to get shook by the hand, and all my friends used to say I was better off being a Protestant because they never shook the Canon by the hand and I did. But apart from that, I could say the Hail Mary off pat in Gaelic and everything. Rattle it out you know. If you were one in four hundred, it's not a problem, when you're fifty in a hundred is when there's a problem.

A Protestant education

When I was at school in Kerry, I started off going to the convent and the Christian Brothers because there was no Protestant school. My family wanted me to have a Protestant education and I got sent to Dublin at twelve, which I didn't like at all. Two hundred and thirty one miles away. I used to hate it. I was homesick for three of the five years. I used to hate it, crawling across the central plain of Ireland in that train that never, ever seemed to get to Dublin.

Great memories of that thing, or ungreat. Great memories when I was going home and ungreat when I was going back.

It was a Methodist school. We had to go to church three times on a Sunday and that's where I developed a very good imagination. I didn't listen to a blind word that he was talking about. I just used to sit there and daydream. That's what I used to do.

A bit of sheep on the hill

I've always been a person who enjoyed the hills and everything like that, I suppose it's like a romantic streak in me, and I was always aware of my surroundings down there. Those places like that were like a world to me down there. I just loved being there. I could go off very easily with friends, we could go swimming all over, in that lake, in that sea, round and about, doing the things that kids would do. A beautiful place to be. You just couldn't ignore it. And it galls me now what's happening to that country with planning corruption and lack of planning. They're destroying it. A headland there, Hog's Back, when I was a kid had one family on it, one farmer who used to get his income from a bit of sheep on the hill and the fishing in the summer. That was the only house out there. Now it's covered in houses. I think eighty per cent are not even Irish. It wouldn't happen over here. It wouldn't be allowed. I couldn't afford to live in my village now. It's cheaper to live here now than it is to live in my village.

I'd probably go back to Ireland before I went to the south of England. I like the Yorkshire people, they tend to be blunt, straight, but there's great humour...it's what you make it. I like the characters I mix with. There's great humour and attitude to life. I think there's similarities with that in Ireland, certainly in Kerry.

"What were you doing last Saturday night?"

I certainly vividly remember one night, there used to be a bar called Brannigans Bar down at the bottom of Briggate. This would have been about '70, '71, and I can remember I had an old Morris Minor which shouldn't have been on the road but was, and I remember being stopped and I was more worried about drink and the condition of my car, but then he said to me, "What were you doing last Saturday night? Where were you?" That was the night of the Birmingham bombings. And I was trying to think, 'Why are they asking me that question?' instead of giving an answer.

The Irish musical capital of Leeds

The sessions at the Victoria finished about four years ago, about 2000, and had been going, I think, for eighteen years. It was in that area of land that I would say was the Irish musical capital of Leeds. It was within a stone's throw of the Old Roscoe, on Sheepscar, next to the Pointers, close to the Regent, the White Stag, and the Eagle, all those pubs. And there was Dizzy and Seamus, they were the landlady and landlord, and they were very, very good. We had musicians in there, but what was nice about it was also that a lot of people just used to meet down there and chat, not necessarily Irish people, they came from all backgrounds. And there was

always music there on a Tuesday night, and very often there was 'afters'. Any travelling musicians who were coming through Leeds knew about the Victoria and would turn up. Some quite big names used to turn up, just turn up in there, or they'd be told to come down, or people would bring them down. So it was a great place and a great shame that it died. With that happening was the closure of a huge chapter of a bar that was known by hundreds of people in Leeds.

Paschal

Paschal was from Roscommon and I think they've gone back there now. He was an All Ireland bodhrán champion. Double jointed wrists. There were things he could do that other people couldn't even hear, with his wrist on the bodhrán.

Harry

Harry used to live up in Woodhouse and I think it was on St. Patrick's Day, every St. Patrick's Day, Harry, who was a big man, used to come down, and he had a cream jacket, cream trousers and a cream panama hat. He used to have a stick, and he had a wonderful bearing. He was a dancer. And he used to walk all the way down from Woodhouse down to the Regent. He was one of these few men who could wear a hat with great dignity and style. Harry. He had the hat on all the time he was in the pub.

133

Gypsy John

One of the best characters I knew or was most closely involved with was called John, or Gypsy John as some of them used to call him. Renowned for not putting his fiddle here, but sticking it on the end of his chin, John originally came from Galway and used to play at fairs in the West of Ireland. Just ordinary fairs, not festivals, just fairs, that's how he used to do it apparently. He was always renowned that he couldn't play a note if he had anything less than two pints in him. If he had between two and six pints he would play brilliantly. And after six pints, forget it. His ritual every Friday was to finish work at Blakey's on Kirkstall Road, and he'd set off and he'd go to the Royal Oak behind the market. He'd play to his mates in there, and then it would depend what sort of state he was in when he got down to the Regent. And we always used to marvel about the fact that he'd go up on the stage and we could never work out how the fiddle stayed on his chin, he stayed on the stool that he was sat on, and the stool, which was usually propped right on the edge of the stage, stayed on the stage. How the whole lot didn't come tumbling — it never did! He wasn't very... what shall we say? He just enjoyed playing and this used to be sometimes at the expense of those around him. If anybody liked a tune he'd just play it and carry on playing it for ages and ages and ages, and then a little few more times after that. He was a great character. I used to give him a lift home sometimes, I always remember on a Friday night, that was half ten closing in Leeds. He lived on Burley Road. We used to go in there and sit in the kitchen, get the fiddles out, his wife would make fried egg sandwiches, tea, and that was it. He had a lovely, lovely touch. All his music was in his head. He had an absolutely gorgeous touch. There were people like him who did inspire me, no two ways about it. It was a treat for me going back to his house. As much as anything else I wanted to go back for him to play because he'd play all night. Play this, play that, play the other.

Mary

Mary was born in 1935 in County Mayo. She emigrated to Leeds in 1953 before returning home to live permanently in 1976 with her husband and children.

The blackest place

I had ventured to Leeds twice with a girl from Wakefield, and I thought it was very big and I thought Boar Lane was black and it looked very black, you see there was a lot of smoke and smog and probably I went on a smoggy day. We went to C&A, we must have saved up a month for clothes, and I remember Boar Lane, 'My God, this is the blackest place.' The buildings were very black at that time and trams were trundling.

Just like we were lost

I always felt hospitals were safe. Loved hospitals. Don't mind hospitals today. So I went up to the Infirmary and got a job at the Infirmary and then my life began! I met a lot more Irish girls, and also there was German girls, Italian girls, Austrian girls. Funnily enough, one German girl tried to teach me German you know, and I had the feeling that they were lost, just like we were lost. A feeling of, 'I wish I could be as good as them', meaning as good as the English girls.

Country clogger

Downtown, you'd go into Lewis's and think, 'I wish I could be as clever and as smart', and even walk like they did. They seemed to walk with a lot of assurance. And this is a horrible thing: I used to be in Boots, and I used to think, 'I wish I was that age, I might then have a bit of—what would you call it—sophistication.' Wasn't that the daftest thing? And the Kardomah coffee place we used to go in, and that used to make me feel really a country clogger 'cos they were older sophisticated girls, women there.

A super way of life

So I worked at the Infirmary then. Got a bit more confidence. Went to every Irish dance there was and lost loads of weight. The Personnel Officer said we'd better have a blood test because of losing so much weight. But I was losing weight because I didn't have time to eat: because there was boys, there was pictures, there was clothes. But it was a super way of life for Irish girls. You were safe. You had a wage. I enjoyed it thoroughly.

It wasn't the done thing

We got married in Leeds in 1958. We got married in St. Anne's Cathedral and lived in a flat off Cardigan Road, and then got a house off Roundhay Road. And then Richard was born. You know, it wasn't the thing for women to work a lot then. You sneaked off to a little job in the hospital maybe two nights a week, two evenings or three evenings, but it wasn't the done thing to plant your child and go.

It was community

The parade was an old-fashioned English
parade. That was Harehills parade. We had
Perkins for bread, you had two good butchers,
you had a lovely greengrocers. They all knew
you. You had a small Tesco's across the road,
you had the Kentucky Fried Chicken. You had
that lovely parade. You had the dry cleaners.
You had the toy shop, the pet shop, you had
a lovely parade. Thirty two years ago. It was
lovely, it was community you see.

The dream

I'd nicely got the contract at the Irish Centre,
good money and I could cope. It was lovely.
Hard, hard work. The Irish Centre was brand
new. Peter was very good and gave a fair
good money. He was a decent man. He's
probably a contractor or retired now. He did
contracting in Leeds and he was the manager
of the Irish Centre at that time. So stayed,
liked it, and got notions. I had a bit of money
then. And my father said, "There's a site,
that field, you can have it, come home."
I was sort of settled. But Dermot, no matter
what you did you couldn't settle him in
England. You could put him down at one
end of Roundhay Park and Dermot would
wander to the other end. He had to keep
going. Streets or gardens were no good to
him. From two, three years of age he wanted
Ireland. So we got this site and Tom came
over and took Dermot with him. That was
thirty years ago. Sometimes had regrets.
There was no work thirty years ago like there
is now. There was no central heating. The
gas fires and the children, it was so difficult.
It's a dream to come home you see, but
believe me, the dream isn't all it's cracked
up to be.

Kathleen

Born in County Mayo in 1939, Kathleen arrived in Leeds aged seventeen to train as a nurse, where she has remained ever since.

It was a beautiful place where I grew up. There was lakes and mountains. We never came in all summer, we just swam and played, helped my father on the farm and helped my mother with the housework. Childhood— full of stories, full of love, full of nature.

My mother was a story-teller

She'd tell us stories at night when she'd be putting us to bed. I suppose to keep us quiet— there was no television. And she'd tell us fantastic fairy stories, like the Blue Magic Cow that came and gave milk to the poor people. She was a fairy cow of course. And her grandfather, all the people round and about said he got information from the fairies, because he could foretell things. Looking back, I suppose he was a man that seen a bit of the future, but he predicted when the big storm was coming, it was like a hurricane that hit Ireland one hundred and fifty years ago maybe. He could also tell about the wars that was coming and the iron horses and bolts in the sky. I suppose he was talking about planes and trains. He also predicted that the Black and Tans would come, and rape and pillage and do all sorts to people. But he'd tell people where to build their houses as well, because you couldn't build on a fairy path. If you did you had to leave both doors open to let the fairies go through. He'd tell you where the best place to set vegetables was, because you always had to leave the path open for the fairies.

My mother also believed, God rest her soul, she also firmly believed in nature. Every single month when the moon would be full coming up over the mountains we had to go to the door and look at it. Same moon, same beauty, the same stillness of the night and the stars, and I can still see it in my mind's eye. To me as a child, it was only come from behind the mountain, but that's where it rose and set. So when I was a bit older I went to the mountain to see if I could look over and see it, but of course the horizon changed all the time when I got there.

The highest mountain in Mayo

I remember the day I left Ireland, I felt excited but scared because I'd never been on a train before. So I said goodbye to my parents and my brothers and sisters which caused me to cry a lot, I was heart-broken really. And I seen the train coming and I thought I should go home really. It was becoming real so. But I didn't. We were both crying, me and my sister, so I got on this train. I was fine while I could see my own place, Nephin, you know, the highest mountain in Mayo, and whilst that was in sight I was fine. But naturally, as the train went on the landscape changed and I realized I was in an alien place with nobody. I sat tight clutching my handbag because I was told, "Don't talk to strangers. Don't let your handbag out of your sight." I thought it was terrible noisy and an awful smell in Dublin. The noise was overwhelming and I just so wanted to be back in my village with my people. But I couldn't go back, I'd made a commitment, I'd said I was going.

137

Keep the faith

We didn't go to English dances because you were told to stay amongst your own, and keep the faith, and we did. I kept what I was brought up to believe in. I have very strong faith. I believe in prayer. And yes, go to Mass. We used to be down at St. Anne's at quarter past six in the morning because we had to be on duty at seven. So we went at quarter past six in the morning, a line of us in nurses' capes, and asleep. We used to be so tired.

Qualify

And then I met my husband. There was a few little Irish dance-halls around Leeds, the Green Room, St. Francis', and the Queen's, and then the Shamrock. My sister had already met the man she married and I met his friend. He was in with them one night in Leeds, they'd come in from working away. We started seeing each other a bit after that but I wasn't keen. Boyfriends weren't so much of a big thing—dancing was. But I didn't like to be with anyone too long. I'd say I'd meet them to go to the pictures and that and I wouldn't turn up. I couldn't be bothered. But anyways he was very persistent. Wherever I went he'd be there. And he said he was madly in love with me. We got engaged. And I remember one of the matrons saying to me, "Don't rush into this." My engagement ring was pinned, because we couldn't wear jewellery on our hands, and she said, she gave me very good advice: "Qualify. You're young, you have plenty of time. Finish your training. Don't rush into marriage." But not much forward thinking. I liked him, he was a good man, and a good dancer, and persistent. So I married him.

The last of the great romantics

I missed freedom. I didn't particularly want to be married. I wanted a white dress. I went back to Ireland to get married, and I wanted the white dress and the big day but then it suddenly dawned on me this was it for life like. And I didn't like that, I didn't like my freedom being so taken. He was a good man, he was a good worker, he wasn't romantic. He didn't suit me. Because I think I was the last of the great romantics, I still had stories in my head, Oisín and Tír na nÓg and all the wondrous things, all the 'knights in shining armour' that would come, but they didn't. Life was too real for that.

I think what we were looking for really was a family here like we had at home. We were looking to create something here for ourselves. Because we were away from our families in Ireland and because there was a terrible void, and insecurity. We tried to create our own little places, you know?

Injustice

Got very involved in the '70s with the politics of Ireland. Cannot stand anything that's unjust. And I was older and wiser then and if I seen the injustice that was done to the Catholics in Northern Ireland, I was there doing anything I could, like after Bloody Sunday, we had a silent vigil down in City Square you know, carrying a candle. It was a silent vigil, but again it was a time I felt very alone because there was people shouting at us. I felt heartbroken for what happened. Totally heartbroken. And the unfairness of it. It had gone on too long. And any way I could support it I would. Then I would speak out, and I would make people understand about the history. I wasn't frightened anymore. I'd never hurt another human being. But I would firmly stand beside my people without fear. It's my love for my country. But that's not saying this country hasn't been very kind and very good to us.

So here I am, fifty years down the line, going home to my niece's wedding in the summer. Still going back on the ferry. Still coming back looking at Ireland.

John

Born in County Mayo in 1937, John worked around Britain for many years before settling in Leeds.

Lakes in the mountain

We had to go to the well for the water. There was lakes in the mountain. You'd get water there. It was cold, summer and winter it was all the same. It was running water. Spring water. It was good water. Made good tea. It was different water than the water you get out of the taps now. You know what I mean? It was real cold. You didn't need to put it into the freezer to get cold. It was cold. If you drank some and you had any holes in your teeth, you'd feel it. Or any tooth-ache, it'd shift the tooth-ache out of you. Because it'd sting you. It was as good as an injection.

A sod of turf

I used to have to walk eight miles to school. In my feet. The lot of us. We had no shoes, no nothing on our feet. And then when we got there in the winter, every one of us, there were four of us going to school, each of us had to bring a sod of turf. Every day we had to bring that sod to make a fire at the school. And all we'd get at school, the meals we had at school was a big mug of cocoa. There was no tea, tea was rationed in our place, you'd get plenty of cocoa and a dry slice of bread, no butter, and that was your lot at the school. And you'd come home at night at half four.

I left school when I was thirteen. I went to Scotland. My father was going. I had a little bag and I had it packed with a few things. He said, "Where are you going?" I said, "I'm going with you to Scotland." He said, "You're not." "Well I am. I'm not going to school no more, I've had enough."

Tattie hokers

The 'tattie hokers' they called us. There was about twelve or fourteen of us. The farmer had a big place, they used to call it 'the bothies'. All men and women used to sleep together and all the kids and everything in a big shed, all the whole lot. And when you'd land there he had big bags, the farmer, and he had a big bale, a big stack of straw, and my father handed me the bag, and I said, "What's the bag for?" He said, "That's your mattress." I says, "Where's my pillow?" He said, "Your jacket." It was a good start off, wasn't it?

Keep the ball rolling

139

Since I came to this country I learned to make me own way: England, Scotland, Wales, all over. Slept out nights, and no money, working here, working there, job finished, and hard to get a job. Sometimes it was a hard time. I used to try and send me parents a little bit of money at home, to me mother, to keep the ball rolling like. I used to look forward to go home to me father and mother for a few months in the winter. We'd get a suit. You might go to a tailor and he'd make a suit for you. It was only a couple of quid. You were tidy as good as you could.

Someone'll shoot me

I had to go back to Ireland for the time being because they were after me for the army. I was only seventeen then. I said, "I'm not going to join any army. If I do, that'll be it. Someone'll shoot me." I went back home to Ireland.

Perished

Well, I have a lot of my time spent now, twenty-four, twenty-five years in Leeds now. I was up in Oakwood for seven years. I was in Gipton for six and a half, and four here. Four or five more years in Chapeltown. I've been out in Beeston. I've been in lots of places. But when I go to a place for a while, unless it's really bad I'm not in a hurry in leaving. I mean, I went up to Oakwood. It was a nice quiet area. But the landlords, they were Indians, they were no good, they had bad flats. Cold, and you were giving the money for nothing. I used to give them £15 every week for heating and I was perished in my place. No right fires or nothing. You'd turn on to have a bath and maybe half way up with your bath your water would turn and go cold. 'Twas no good, no.

The drink

I was on the drink here for about three months. It's nearly three years ago now. I haven't a drink since. And I was very bad here. Falling, and I couldn't hardly move. I travelled years ago, coming and going here and boozing there. Maybe drank out on a bench different days, trying to meet company because I had no-one to talk to and this and that, and sometimes you wouldn't meet good ones out there, neither.

I go to Delaney's, "What are you having John, a pint of Stones?" when I'm off the drink, but when I was drinking they wouldn't ask me for a drink. Some of them don't want to see me going well. They don't want to see me off the drink. They want to get me going, and get a laugh out of me and have a bit of a joke and a craic.

If I go into a pub and start drinking pints, I'm not one that'll come up with one or two pints. I'll come up maybe when I'm drunk. If I go in at 11 o'clock in the morning and I have money, I'll come up then at maybe 11 o'clock at night and I'm put out.

Go my own way

I go down town sometimes when I get fed up and I jump on a bus. I go to Halifax and I go to Keighley, I go to Huddersfield, I go to different places, and I go up to Crossgates. I meet a man there, he's an old fella from Donegal. I go in there and me and him do be sorting out a few horses and a bit of chat, he's a nice old man. In fairness, one thing about it, I'm fairly well liked out there because I'm the type that never falls out with people. If I get in a bad mood for a day—it's very rare I do—if I do, I'll go and sort it out myself. Go my own way.

I couldn't get on with the euros. I'm sixty-eight years of age now and I don't feel like going to Ireland now. I'm so long here.

Tommy

Manager of the Leeds Irish Centre for thirty years, Tommy was born near Stoke-on-Trent in 1941 of Mayo parents.

Backlash

It was very difficult,'74,'75, very, very difficult here because that's when the Northern Ireland thing started to sort of erupt, and there was a backlash here, obviously. It was constant phone calls.

Then you would get the odd bomb scare. You'd get this telephone call, and sometimes they'd be the police and they'd say, "This is genuine because it's coded." There'd be certain codes, you see, that you knew were genuine and you'd have to empty the place. I remember sitting in here, the week that Lord Mountbatten died, and we had to close the curtains, and we just had to sit in darkness.

I think what we started to do really from then on was to involve ourselves in the community. Because we hadn't done a lot within the community, to be fair. I remember when the idea came up for the Lord Mayor's Parade. It was my idea and a couple of others and we went for it, and do you know it was absolutely brilliant. I thought to myself, 'Whatever happens they're not going to abuse kiddies.' So we filled the float with kiddies. Irish dancing and little kiddies playing music, and off it went, and we won, we won a prize, believe it or not!

Going away

One of the most poignant things I ever saw, it was 1951, we were at home on holidays, and I stood on the platform with my mother, I was coming back home. But to see all youngsters leaving home, you know it stayed with me forever that. I saw these waiting for the train, mother and father with a daughter, mother and father with a son, and these were going away, going to England, and never been on a train before, you can imagine can't you?

Fair play

You can be lucky and you can be in the right place at the right time, that type of thing. And there was a lot of fellas when the building boom was on, took the chance and bought a machine or got a job, self-employed type thing. But fair play to them, they were willing to do that. A lot of other lads were a little bit more conservative, you know, 'I've got a wife and family, I can't really afford to do that.' And they carry on working. There's a lot of people who've done very well, fair play to them, you know.

I was so annoyed when I used to go to Ireland and, "He's English," but if there was a person over from America, "Oh, Irish American." My equivalent in America was always Irish American, but you come from England, and it used to bug me.

141

Be myself

When I was about nineteen I used to sing a little bit. I was picked up in Ireland by the Americans to go to America. This 'new voice,' or whatever. I didn't know what they were going to do with me. I was supposed to go to Chicago, but anyway the whole thing was set up but I had to have an Irish passport. And I had to be Irish, I couldn't be what I was. And the more I thought of this, the more I thought, 'I can't go. I can't go there.' It was in the papers here and all, whatever. I thought, 'I can't go to Chicago. What if I'm singing in a place one night and someone comes up to me and said, "Where are you actually from?" And even if I say mother's place, Midfield, "Oh do you know such and such?" I thought I don't want to be caught out like that. I don't want to lie. I want to be myself. So I never went. So I went to London then.

I just wrote

I worked in construction. On the buildings. A good job, a great job. I was in charge, I was a ganger man, I was in charge of this high rise of flats, and, of course, it was good money at the time. And the next thing was that this job was advertised—Manager of the Leeds Irish Centre. And people said, "Why don't you?" and I wouldn't, anyway mother said, "Why don't you?" and I just wrote. I used to be involved in the old club, you know I used to get up and sing a song and that type of thing, so when my application came along they said, "Look if we don't give him an interview the people will go mad, they'll think it's a set up." Because they had these other managers coming from Birmingham and different places. And, of course, the guy that was supposed to be the favourite, when he came along, I think his demands were a little bit more than what they anticipated, and they thought, 'My God, who else is there?' And it was me, and that's it. It was strange really. And when I came in I thought I'd made the biggest mistake of my life. I thought, 'Well, I must stay here for at least six months for shame's sake,' and I couldn't believe it. I'd been to the place a good few times, obviously, and to me it was booming, but financially when I came in it was something else.

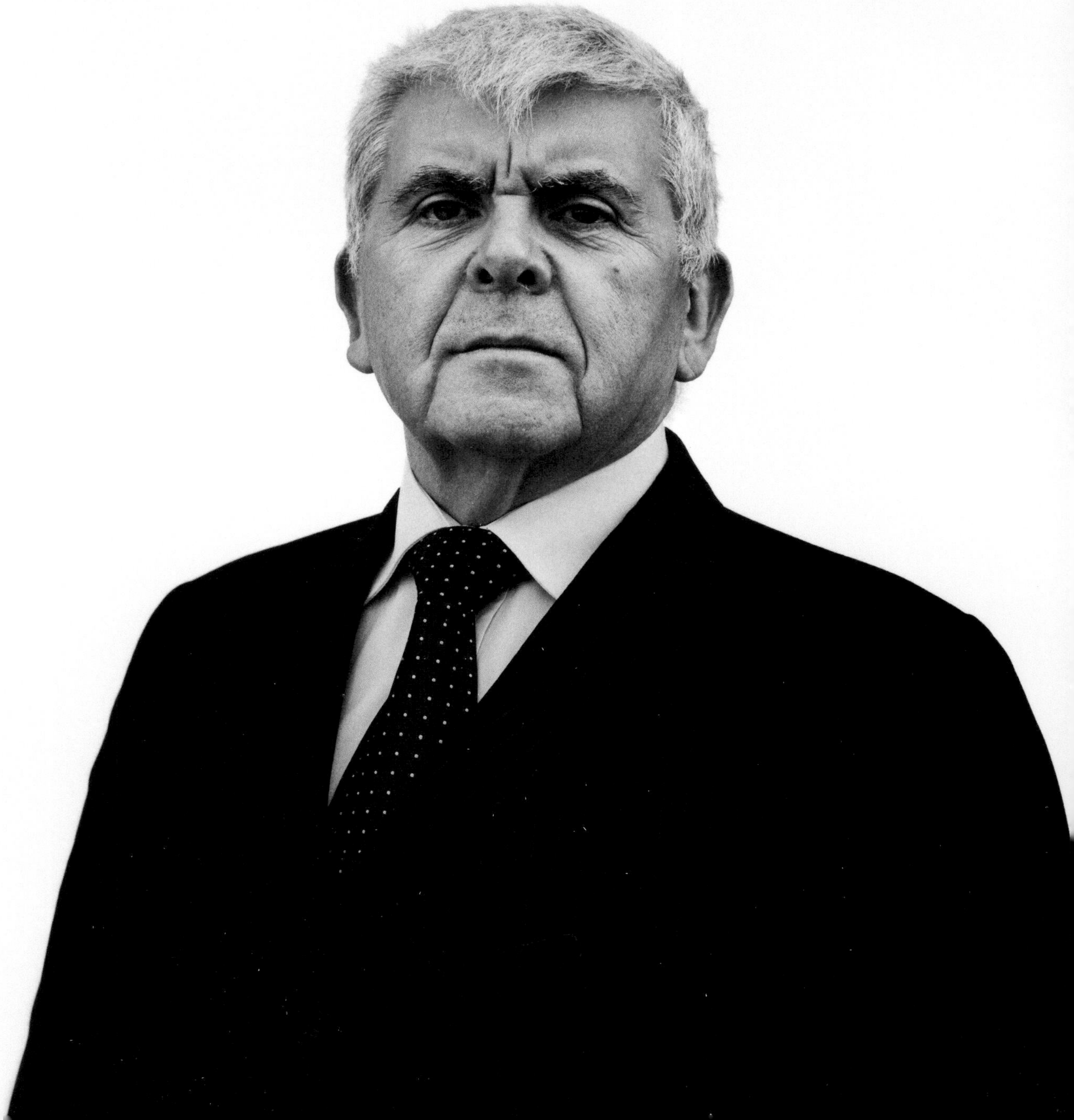

Richard

Richard was born in 1940 in County Mayo and emigrated to Leeds at the age of nine. After working in construction for many years, Richard became the manager of Davitt House, a residential home for older Irish people in Leeds. He has recently retired.

Nine years of age I was. We left Ireland on 16th September, 1949, it was a Friday. We come over, the boat was The Princess Maud. It used to take cattle as well. You got off at Holyhead and you had to get on a train from Holyhead to Chester, change at Chester to Manchester, change at Manchester to Leeds. It was awful daunting, long, it was like twenty four hours it was.

The naivety
On the first day in Leeds, we'd been down to St. Anne's Mass at eleven o'clock in the morning, and we were walking out, and I seen this black man across the other side of the road, and I had never seen a black man in my life. And just think, I was nine years of age then. And I shouted, "Oh, auntie, look, a black man, a black man." And next thing, I got my ear pulled. And looking back now, there's thousands of them here, but in them days I didn't know such a thing existed. That was the naivety from rural Ireland.

I've still got the 1949 penny that I brought over with me, to this day. I keep it in a drawer. It's travelled all over all these years so it's along fifty-five years travelling with me.

Sandwiches for the lads
Our house was a lodging house and we used to take boarders, Irish lads that had come over. It was £1.10s in those days and then it went up to £2.0 a week, full board. That was packing a lunch for them as well, sandwiches for the lads that worked in the construction industry. There used to be eight or nine or ten lads in our house. They used to get their remittance, go down to the post office and send money home, a pound or two pounds, or whatever they could afford. But what they used to do, some of them, to avoid paying a lot of income tax, they used to have a false name of somebody who was a neighbour at home who was probably forty or fifty years of age and had a load of children. I always remember this lad, he was about nineteen, and he maintained he had five children and he was married to Mary Ellen something, and all the names of the children were written up so that he knew what to write on the tax form.

Money
I started work 15th April, 1955, which makes me fifty years working. I was an apprentice and my wage was £1.9.10d. That's less than £1.50 a week. Money was very small. My brother come over about 1958 from Ireland, and he come to live with my aunt. I'd been going to night-school, you had to go for your City and Guilds, so I went for that and done three years at college. So my brother came over and he went straight out on construction, on the buildings. And he was getting three times the amount of money that I was. And I felt a bit peeved that I'm going to night-school and everything, going through an apprenticeship and he come and done all that hard work that was more menial and not as technical as what I was doing, and getting three or four times the amount of money.

Well, I had so little money that if you met a nice girl you couldn't afford to take her out. Well he could, and he could flash money around, and I couldn't. So I thought, 'To heck with this.' I then packed in my trade and everything and went out and worked on the construction. And I did that for the next thirty years. And I done well out of it, because I got good money and I travelled all over. If I lived my life again I wouldn't have changed it for the world, that part of it.

A great pride
You'd have to be awful lazy to be out of work. There was the high rise flats going on, and an abundance of buildings going on, because that period after the war was the building up of the cities, the network of roads and new towns, so you just completely transformed every place. From the Leeds of fifty years ago to today, from being a dark, dank old place, it's now a vibrant city. And the Irish can take a great pride from that. You worked on that, and you'd feel that's part of you there and part of your time.

"I'll give her a dance"

I met my wife Betty, she's from Sligo, 23rd August, 1962. It was a Wednesday and there was a band from Ireland. I'd been dancing with this girl, and she said, "Oh my friend would like to have a dance with you." "Oh, who's your friend?" So she said, "That girl that's over there in the red skirt and white blouse, and white shoes." So I looked across and I seen that she was about three inches or more taller than me. So I said to her, "If you tell her to take off her shoes, I'll give her a dance." In them days there were three bars to the dance, there was the quickstep, the waltz and the foxtrot, and after that you'd disperse and the girls all went over to the one side and the men to the other side. After that girl went over I could see them having a big giggle. Anyway the music started off again for the next dance, and I thought, 'Well, will I be brave here and go over and ask her or what?' Anyway I thought, 'I'll chance my arm.' She was a good looking girl and I thought, 'She's too good for me.' Anyway, she said 'Yes.' Going down through the crowd she held my hand tight, and I thought, 'I'm getting somewhere here.' I thought, 'Oh, I've made it here.' We've been together ever since. We courted for two years, and married on 29th August, 1964. So we've just celebrated our Ruby Wedding. So I've always been looking up. I always thought I'd bring some height into the family. I didn't want my kids to be as small as me.

Improve and move

I always say you should improve and move. I've moved about four or five times since the first house, and I've always got the highest price in the street every time I sold. Improve yourself. When the Irish come over in the '40s and '50s, there's polarization, they all come to each other, and you're in like a ghetto. But then you've got to move out from that, expand out from that. Everybody's got to start off somewhere. But then you've got to move on and do your own thing.

A step or two on the ladder

The Irish had moved up from being not wanted. It fell to the West Indian community that they wasn't liked, and the Irish got up a step or two on the ladder. It was like Enoch Powell wanted all the West Indians to be sent back home, and the Irish moved up a step, you see. But then with the Troubles starting in Northern Ireland, that brought us back down again. What we had gained, we had lost. And we had to keep our heads below the parapet for a long time, with the bombings on the mainland. You did have to keep quiet, and you couldn't express yourself like you started to express yourself in the late '60s. But now, thankfully, again we've overridden that.

The younger Irish could come together and meet the needs of these elderly Irish. Give them a sense of purpose in life, in the latter years of life. Not feel that they're left on the shelf, you know, unwanted. And I think we all owe it to them to foster that good will for them. The biggest thing is when people are alone, then bitterness creeps into their thoughts and minds, that probably they took a wrong turn in life and it hasn't panned out as they had hoped.

Patricia

Patricia was born in England. Her father was from County Tipperary, and her mother's grandfather came from County Cork.

I was born in Yorkshire, and I'm very, very proud of Yorkshire, and when people talk about Leeds, that the Industrial Revolution clad the world, made all the uniforms for the First World War, I really feel proud of Leeds. They had the Lancaster bomber. There's so much about Leeds that I'm very, very proud of. And when we were doing an evening class on the Industrial Revolution, and I thought, 'I'm part of this' I felt so proud to be Leeds. But yet, I'm Irish as well.

Ireland on the map
I was in America for a while. When I first went to America, the girls in the office where I worked would be saying, "Oh, you're Irish. My great-grandfather came from County Cork. Do you know him?" Or, "Do you know the family?" They look at Ireland on the map, and it's such a tiny dot, compared with the States, that they think everybody must know everybody else. They practically do, mind. At least they did when I was young. It was like a medieval English village, people didn't move, they stayed in their own area.

Sweet and innocent
My uncle John, my father's favourite brother, had only ever been to Dublin for the hurling matches, until his son married in England and he was over for the first time. Now this I thought was rather sweet and innocent. Uncle John lived in the village. And he'd worked all his life and never met any English people. I mean we weren't counted as English—they accepted my mother because she could go on and sing all the rebel songs, which she did frequently. And Uncle John came and said, "I got the train, and there was this English man sitting on the train. And he was very nice. He was very friendly." I don't know if he thought he was going to get stabbed in the back or what. But he couldn't get over it. Poor Uncle John.

The Irish have a potential to do well. They have the wit, they seem to have the imagination, and they don't obey the rules.

Bernard

Born in Leeds in 1958, of parents from County Cavan, Bernard was responsible for writing the first ever statistical report on the modern Irish community in Leeds based on the 1981 Census, which was instrumental in changing Leeds City Council's ethnic monitoring policies.

Everything tasted of peat

When I was a kid and we went over, there was no running water in the house, no toilet, no electricity. Everything was cooked on the fire so everything tasted of peat. You got used to that after a day: tea, custard, potatoes, everything. If you wanted water we'd go down to the lake with my uncle, he had an ass and a cart. So we'd go down, there were oil lamps on the walls, there was a radio and that was it. And that's where we spent our holidays. Like most places, Gowna was a one-horse town. There was a crossroads and still there's three pubs, a post office, a general store, there was two general stores, and that was it, and obviously houses. You could walk through it in about two minutes.

The Mayo mafia

In most places there's one or two counties predominate, and maybe it's true everywhere, I don't know. But in Leeds, if you take Mayo, I remember mum and dad, especially my dad who worked on the buildings, and they used to go on about the Mayo mafia. You used to find it on the buildings. And my mother used to say if you weren't in the ring, if you weren't from Mayo, that's it. So these guys would look after people from Mayo and if you weren't from Mayo, then bugger off basically.

Emigré politics

I was on the committee of the Comhaltas at one point. I've been on the committee for virtually everything. I was involved with that in the first year, then unfortunately, like an awful lot of things I've been involved in, to a degree, not all but a lot of Irish things degenerate into what I call 'émigré politics', which is, it fractures into personalities and in-fighting, and that's basically what began to happen to that.

Ethnic monitoring

This would have been the early eighties. A Polish friend of mine was on the Ethnic Minorities, and he said the Irish should be involved. The Irish Centre committee said, "You go and represent the Centre." So I got involved with that, and the first thing I discovered was that they'd done a survey of the workforce for Leeds City Council. And it was so specific that it even identified people like Americans and Phillipinos. Not one Irish person, according to their data, was employed by the Council. Now obviously there were Irish people working for the Council, so I was curious, why aren't they in the statistics? I got in contact with the Irish Post. They did a huge article, 'No Irish in Leeds.' It appeared that Leeds City Council were discriminating against the Irish. So they began to suddenly realise they had better start taking the Irish seriously. The Irish weren't just going to fade into the background. And they did this report based on the census of the Afro-Caribbeans, the Asians and everybody else in Leeds in

terms of socio-economic profiles. I did
my own research in the Council Planning
Department and a report, and discovered
that the profile of the Irish in Leeds was very
similar to that of the black ethnic minorities.
The Council were quite shocked actually
because I'd done it, and also because
suddenly I'm saying the Irish had got a
similar profile in terms of: the elderly were in
the inner city, they're alone, they're culturally
isolated. They had this stupid category of
what did they call it? 'UK Irish' or 'British Irish,'
or some nonsensical thing. So they agreed
then that they would actually have 'Irish' as
a category for ethnic monitoring purposes
in Leeds.

Ignorance

When I was Federation of Irish Societies
Education Officer I did a critique on the Swan
Report, which was multi-cultural education.
It's a book about four or five inches thick.
There were two references to the Irish in that
entire thing. And it starts off with a definition
of prejudice. 'Prejudice is defined as being
based upon ignorance.' So I then based my
whole critique by saying the people on the
Swan committee are guilty of the same thing
they accuse everybody else of – ignorance.
Did they consider the Irish? No. Completely
ignorant. So I wrote a paper on the idea of
the inclusion of the Irish in any multi-cultural
education policy. I got requests for that
from all around the world. The Japanese
Department of Education wanted one. I also
got requests from Australia, America and
all over Britain as well.

Rachel

Born in 1977, Rachel was brought up in
Leeds by Mayo parents.

Stride the land

My father's home place is still very much a
home. It's where my uncles live, it's an active
farm, it's very much the way he grew up on
it. And he identifies very, very strongly with
the land. That's always been what we've
considered our home place to be. My dad
feels very strongly about his roots. Not so
much his roots as where he belongs. And the
first thing he would always do when we got
home was walk out and stride the land. And
that's what me and my brothers do when we
go, with or without my parents, we get out
and we walk on the land. Because that's what
we were taught 'home' was.

A place in time

I think all places are a place in time. You can't
have one without the other. And so when my
mum in particular, talks about her home, her
home place, she talks about being a younger
woman, about her and her sisters when they
were going out to dances. The freedom that
they had in their lives, to cycle six miles to
a dance on a night-time and come back not
so late that their daddy would be cross with
them, but late enough to let them feel they
were doing something exciting. All of that is
gone and I don't think they would get that
back anywhere. I don't think they would want
it back either, because certainly my mother
wouldn't cycle anywhere these days.

History

My mother is a great story-teller and so are
her family. One of my really distinct memories
from childhood is sitting on the floor
because all the adults were sat on the seats,
and you know, maybe a visitor was coming
from Ireland or from another part of Leeds
and that was a big event, and it meant
that you sat around and you told stories.
My mother's stories were of people of maybe
one or two generations before her from her
village, as well as her own family stories, and
things that happened to her as a child, and
even things that happened maybe only a year
or so ago. You know, you would say, "Mum
tell me again the time Christopher came home
from the hospital." And that was how history
was passed on.

The story you're telling

My Uncle John in Ireland, he's another great
story-teller, and he definitely doesn't let the
truth get in the way of a really good story. But
at the same time it's almost a truer rendition
of it because it's his memory of it. It's the way
he saw it and the way people around him
saw it and the re-telling of it, and I think I've
adapted to their way of telling stories to the
way I tell stories and the way I see things. It's
a continuation, it's who you are by telling the
story as well as the story you're telling.

149

A longer lasting legacy

My dad, he's into the Gaelic football, he
works with St. Anthony's Gaels, and he says
that the level of quality of play is actually
decreasing because there isn't the new
generation coming to raise the level up.
On the other hand, I was saying to him, the
fact that kids are playing it at all, the fact
that you are getting young Asian kids coming
over from the other side of Beeston and
saying, "What are you playing? Can we play
with you?" is brilliant. That's a longer lasting
legacy, that other people get to touch and
feel something about Ireland.

A community

There are a lot of people I know of Irish origin
who work in the voluntary community sector.
I think that's to do with the fact that we were
raised by a community that has an awareness
of looking after its neighbours. There are
people of Irish origin who are doing incredibly
well in business, because they were taught
to work hard, to do well, to be successful, and
to push beyond the boundaries, and I think
more so than people without that identity.
Those are things I'd like to see us celebrating.
Not just drinking.

My mum always says, "Oh, there's no dances
any more." Which might be a lot to do with
how times have changed, but still that constant
checking in with everybody else seems to
have been lost. I wonder how much of that
is because of assimilation and because of the
spreading out across the city as opposed to
being in one enclave any more.

I would say I'm from Leeds very, very strongly,
but culturally I would say I'm Irish. And if you
would really like to know, I'd say I'm Leeds
Irish, or Beeston Irish, that's who I am.

Paddy

Paddy, born in 1927 in County Clare, is President of the Yorkshire Gaelic Athletic Association and Chairman of O'Neill's Gaelic Football Club.

There was nothing for me. There was nothing for me. I was second oldest of sixteen.

Coming every week in batches
I came here in August 1947. I was twenty. I came over to the mines, that was the only way you could get over. You had to sign on to go to the mines. They paid my fare. At the Labour Exchange they had an agent that interviewed you to see whether you were suitable. There was a crowd of us, about twenty-two of us. But they were all from different parts of Ireland. I would imagine they were coming every week in batches.

I could have cried
Leeds was very different. I remember going home on holidays about eighteen months afterwards, and coming back to Leeds and getting out of Leeds city station and the fog and everything was… I could have cried, to be quite truthful, I could have gone back again.

If I talk Irish I get angry
There was nothing, only the boat, and that was sad. And we weren't prepared at school for the boat or for emigration. I did feel angry and I told them so. And when you came over here you just had to get books again and start learning the best way you could. Night school. I spent a time at night school. I can count better in Gaelic, that's the only thing I can do. If I talk Irish I get angry. When I think about it I just get angry.

That's their Wembley
The young lads they're togged out, and they run out on that field and they feel right proud and they give their best. They absolutely play their hearts out. And the crowd is there to watch them in a big stand, you know. Brings out the best in them. That's their Wembley.

Today you have to keep fit. Fitness today is a great want. There's a lot of money today spent in fitness. Whatever better way to get rid of a few pounds than playing Gaelic football?

When they get to sixteen and eighteen they think they're men. They have money then, they have jobs, you know supermarkets, shops, and all sorts, they're working the weekends and the evenings and they have money. They don't be interested in football then. Very few of them.

They were great, they were a great team, O'Neill's were. O'Neill's had the Mones, three Mones. Tony, Kevin was a terrier, that's the only way I can describe him. Put that ball all over the place. It was great. Philip was a beautiful player, a fine player.

Paddy

The St. Colmcille Association

It was formed in 1956 by Canon Stritch and that was for people coming over. The aims of the organisation was to get work and get lodgings and to help people, particularly young women. Today, Leeds is a beautiful place. But going back in the 1950s and early '60s, there was a lot of poverty in Leeds. A lot of poverty. I've seen them coming to the Oxford Row office, getting vouchers, and they used to take them to Belle View Road to a shop-keeper and she would give them the value of the voucher in goods. And if they wanted money she would just tear up the voucher in front of them. That was it. She wouldn't give them no money, they come for food. They couldn't buy clothing there, it was food only. Everything to do with the table.

Dead or alive

I got a massive heart attack in 1985. I had a triple by-pass. My niece was getting married in Ireland and I got the hard word. They said I had to go, dead or alive! I went. The doctors arranged for oxygen to be picked up in Ireland and all this medicine. I went to Ireland and we went to the wedding and then I went down to the West Coast. I went to Knock shrine in County Mayo. I went to Knock and after that I was okay. I just went and prayed. That's all. So I've been back to Knock every year since. So I haven't an ache or a pain or nothing ever since.

'Brave Irish Man Stops Runaway Horse'

In 1948 I was coming home from work at half past two and it was August. There was a hullabaloo in the Headrow and all the crowd was looking, had stopped, and all of a sudden this horse appeared by the Town Hall with the shafts of its cart tied onto the harness. And they were out like that, flying at the other side of the horse. And it came along the Headrow. I seen a woman with a pram in front of it, you know. She was stuck to the ground with fright. So when it was passing me I just jumped on it and I caught it by the mane and I got my hand up its nose and I turned it upside down in the middle of the road. And then the policeman came on a horse. We got the horse up off the road and I had still a hold of it. Then the man came ten minutes afterwards with his cap in his hand, all sweating, and he got the horse calmed down and took it away. That was at half past two. And at half past three my name was on the front page of the Evening Post and it says, 'Brave Irish Man Stops Runaway Horse.' So I was taken to the Town Hall for a mug of tea and we had a chat down there, you know. So then this bloke, this councillor from the Town Hall called Sidney Porter or something, he came, and he was like a father to me. He was right nice. About six weeks afterwards he brought me to the Civic Hall to meet Lady Masham. And she gave me a what-do-you-call it, a certificate of bravery and £10. It was a lot of money in those days. And the certificate, didn't I lose it? If I only had it now I could show it to my children and my grandchildren, and they could have it. It would be just great. But being in lodgings and moving from one place to the other, I just mislaid it somewhere.

Jackie

Jackie was born in County Roscommon and emigrated when he was a teenager. He is Vice-Chairman of the Leeds branch of Comhaltas Ceoltóirí Éireann after having been Chairman for thirty years.

I did not like it here. Did not like it at all. God, I did not like it. I absolutely hated it. I'll never forget the smell in the room the first morning I woke, and of course it was soot and sulphur. I woke up and there was this horrendous smell. I thought, 'What the hell's that?' My nose was running black, honest to God. I was absolutely devastated. I couldn't believe that life could have got so bad.

I won't be seeing you again

I was quite young when I came over. I'd be about seventeen and a half, eighteen. What prompted me? Everyone was coming, but I wasn't going to come to England. And I wasn't. I had no intentions of going to England. No-one expected me to go to England. And then my mother, the Lord be with her, went on holiday, and I suddenly thought, 'It's going to be very difficult to go to England with my mother here. So I'll go when she's on holiday.' So that was that, that was the decision. So she was on holiday, I went to England. 'Twas the easiest. T'would have been… I knew it would be hard. And I remember coming home from work and I thought, "I'm going to England tomorrow." I said to my father, "I'm going to England tomorrow." He said, "Well, that's sudden." And that was it. Next day I went in to the little town, Frenchpark and told them, and nobody believed me, they thought I was joking because everybody used to talk about it and talk about it for months and months or a year before they'd go, and I never mentioned England, the word never crossed my lips. And I said, "I won't be seeing you again, I'm off to England in the morning." And I went.

A grand player

Music has always been in my life. When I was a young lad, every Sunday we'd go across to my grandfather's, and the Sunday evening after the tea, the neighbours would come in, we'd be only kids, and they'd be dancing the sets and the lads and my grandmother they'd be playing. Everyone has a bodhrán nowadays, but when I was growing up the only people who had a bodhrán was our family, and my grandfather used to kill the goats and skin them and put the skin in the lime pit and cure it. And he made his own bodhráns. We were the only ones who played them. Now every other one's playing a bodhrán.

Grandmother was one of these people who, if you went in the evening as a young lad, she'd be there and she'd have everything done and cleaned up and she'd say, "I'll play you a little tune." She'd get the accordion now and she'd play for you in the middle of the day. She was smashing.

One of the things that my mother used to do that you remember now was my dad would go out rambling, and she'd be making the beds and she'd start singing and she was a great singer. And then she had us all round and we'd all sing.

Comhaltas Ceoltóirí Éireann

Comhaltas was a movement I was aware of
before I left Ireland. I was never involved in it
but I was aware of it. Irish music in those days
was only played in the kitchens. And all the
dance-halls were what my father and mother
would say the 'modern dance-halls,' because
in their day, that's not going back so far, it was
the crossroad dance. They met in the village,
and went to the crossroads, and the musicians
played at the dance. Then what they called
the modern dances and dance halls started to
come in, and then you had the modern bands,
playing all the modern music, and I grew up
with that as well. So Irish music took a back
seat, at a carnival and that there'd be one céili
and that'd be on a night when the youngsters
wouldn't go, that was for the old fogeys. So
Irish music had very much taken a back seat.
I mean, I knew players who had hung their
fiddles up and didn't play any more unless
they wanted to play for themselves, no-one
was listening anymore. And then that is the
one thing Comhaltas did do, it brought the
traditional Irish music in, in an organised
fashion and suddenly gave it a new lease of
life.

Undefeated

John must get the credit for starting the branch.
He got so enthusiastic about it. In Leeds at
that time you had Michael. Now Michael was
not just a player, he was a grand singer as well.
And then there was Joe and Pat, and they
were lovely men. And there were others like
them at the time. In '69, we started the branch
of Comhaltis and started teaching youngsters.
I think that was the big thing—for the first
time young people started being taught the
music. And Leeds sort of took off on that. In the
early days John became All Ireland champion,

a brilliant player. Two or three times he was
asked to retire, undefeated. They were asked
to retire then because they could have won it
four times or five times. It would get silly.

The elite

It was a great time for the Comhaltis
movement because it was fresh. In those
days at the fleadhs there would be thousands
at them. Leeds became the most successful
branch by a mile in the whole of the
Comhaltis movement, and then gradually
played a part that was important in the
community and the Irish Centre. It became
known as the elite when it came to producing
scóraíchts. I suppose there was great
dedication.

Sometimes you lost a lot of people
going back to Ireland—to emigration!
I never thought I'd be saying it. Emigration
is ruling us. We lost families, whole families
back to Ireland. Half our branch is in Ireland,
dotted around the place.

People got a lot out of it. And nine out
of ten gave something back. That shows how
much they liked it. The pupil became the
teacher, and that has been the story of the
Leeds branch.

You must change

If you're going to keep up with the times, keep
going ahead, you've got to change. It was
a culture shock from being involved with
such a nice friendly atmosphere within the
Comhaltis movement to get involved with other
groups who didn't actually work together
like that. You must change. There's no such
thing as stopping still, you get left behind.
I found that that was the biggest drawback,
trying to introduce new things, new ideas.

Frank

Born in County Mayo in 1936, Frank emigrated from Ireland to Wigan in Lancashire on his seventeenth birthday. He is Chairman of the Leeds Mayo Association.

The Leeds Mayo Association

Maureen is secretary, Paddy, there was a big committee of us. But it's like everything else, they just dwindle away. There are just two or three of us keeping it going now. It's the same with the St. Patrick's Parade, we had a meeting there the other night and there was only four or five of us. And they criticise you about not having this and not having that and not having the other, and then half of them won't go to the trouble of marching in it when the day comes after all the work you've put in. They just think you can do what you like but you can't. You have to get permission from the police, it's unbelievable the amount of work that goes into it…unbelievable. We get a grant off the Council, five or five and a half thousand, which goes nowhere, as you would appreciate. I mean the year before last we had the Artane Boys Band over from Dublin. Well, they don't come cheap.

If we were to rely on me own people we could forget about it. We have as many English people as Irish people at the dinner dances. But we're still, you know, having a very successful dinner dance every year. Shoving up near on three hundred people which I still consider a very, very good function.

Leeds Irish Centre

There's five or six different groups I know that I would safely say over the past fifteen, sixteen years, they've sat at the same tables, the self same table, night after night. Doesn't make sense to me. They'll get very upset if there are strangers sitting at it. Get very upset in fact.

Over there

Everything is more modernised now. Houses, big big houses. That's something I can't understand about them over there, these five and six bedroom houses and just a couple of them living in it. Two and three bathrooms and toilets. The maintenance of them and the heating, it must be colossal. Throwing away money for nothing for the sake of this big mansion. There's only one room you can sleep in, isn't there?

'Twas them that were speaking fast

'Twas hard sometimes to understand some of them, especially the Yorkshire people. Because you've got so many different accents, especially if you go out Barnsley way. They'd just say, "Will you speak slowly, we can't understand you." You would think 'twould be the other way around. 'Twas them that were speaking fast, me that was speaking slow.

The Irish passport

They were a hellish drawback when I came here if you went out abroad. You know, on holidays with the Irish passport. You were left, and all the rest went through and they were boarding the 'plane and the whole issue. And you were kept back and they were checking it all and I don't know, you just felt a bit out of it. Cause you had all the Troubles then, you know. So with the result I got an English passport 'cause you were entitled to it after you were here for so many years. That solved that problem. Probably if I got the chance now I'd go back to it, but I cannot go back to the Irish passport.

Of course I worked

There was nothing in Ireland for me. I made me home here. I've got a reasonable life. I were never out of work, never short of a few shillings. I mean, there was probably a lot of people not as fortunate as me, but if you were prepared to work… I've had that argument with people. They says, "Well you worked." Of course I worked for what I got. If you don't work you don't get it no matter what country you're in.

Horse work

I retired when I were sixty-two and I had enough. When you're working six and seven days a week all your life you think, 'O God!' I have seen a lot of my mates, they retired at sixty-five, they were dead at sixty-six, sixty-seven. Of course it takes its toll out of you. Cause some of them worked bloody hard, you know what I mean? I mean these lads had been out digging trenches and putting cable in, and all that was horse work was that.

Green Guinness

The second generation Irish, they're not as Irish as what the Irish in America are, are they? I mean Christ Almighty, in America if there's a bit of Irish going back five or six generations, they're Irish through and through aren't they? They even turn around and make green Guinness on St Patrick's Day there and the whole issue. Unbelievable, unbelievable. I don't know. It makes you wonder.

Frank

Sarah

Senior Midwife at St. James's Hospital, Sarah emigrated from County Mayo to Leeds in 1970 when she was eighteen.

When I was in school in Castlebar, there was never any idea that as a girl you would go to University. That wasn't thought of. So you did the exams for the Civil Service or you did the exams for the bank or you did nursing. And I wasn't getting on very well with maths at all, so it was going to be nursing. There was no such thing as, 'Did you want to go nursing?'

Red brick

There was me and my friend Mary, and they met us at Leeds Bradford airport and took us into the hospital and took us to the nurses' home. They told us the direction of where the dining room was, and that was it. That was just totally it! And we went to bed, we each had our little rooms, like little nuns' cells. And we got up the next morning and came out, and we walked down as far as you know, St. Patrick's Church, it's closed up now, and all I can remember thinking, 'The whole of England is made of red brick. There is nothing else but red brick. Why couldn't they think of something else?' And we went to Mass at St. Patrick's Church and came back up to the hospital again, and I thought that was the whole of Leeds. We'd seen all of Leeds. We didn't know there was another bit, further on, in town you know.

160

Irish soil

Most people I think, when they get to a certain age, they've got married and they've got children, and the children are growing up, will say, "Well, this is my home now." I don't think I will ever be like that. There is some part of me that only feels totally comfortable when I'm standing on Irish soil. It is not anything about the difference between Ireland and England. It is the place I grew up. It's not about Mayo, it doesn't have to be Mayo, it's something about the island of Ireland. When I am on the island of Ireland I feel more at peace within myself.

I remember one time when I would go to Ireland for a fortnight and have a lovely time and come back and feel quite depressed and… not lonely, but depressed and claustrophobic almost, in Leeds. And I can remember being standing over there at the kitchen sink and looking out the window, and what I miss, and I worked it out, is seeing the horizon. When you live in a city you never, ever see the horizon.

Kathleen, may she rest in peace, said I was to come to Leeds because it was less frightening and less busy than London. But she never mentioned that it was so far from the sea, and I would have much preferred to have been nearer the sea. Because when you're in any part of Ireland, almost, you're near the sea.

If I want in my mind to find if I'm upset or, I won't say lonely, because I'm not a lonely kind of a person because I'm quite good at being alone anyway, but if I have any worries or problems, if I can picture in my mind's eye the beach in Inniscrone it brings me a certain peace.

I would say if you looked back over the last fifty years and could identify all the Irish women and men that came over, there would be more men that became isolated, lonely, alcoholics and went the wrong way. There would be far more men than women. But I think that's because women are better at coping and better at improving the quality of their life.

Tough!

We were talking about what we would do when we would qualify, when you'd finish your training. And I can't remember what I said, because I had certainly no plan, but one of the other girls that was Irish said that she was hoping to go back to Ireland. And the Sister was very scathing, and said, "Oh, yes! You come over here, to get our good training and then scarper off." As if we were making use of the facility of working in St. James's. And I said, "Hang on! We've worked for our training. We worked damned hard, forty hours a week. You used us as hands-on." We weren't just sitting on our bottoms being educated. We worked and worked hard. We got a pittance of a wage, we didn't have enough to survive on, we certainly didn't. I mean, your mind-set when you left Ireland was that you had left and you weren't going back. And you were expected to do well. So, if you were homesick, tough! If you were broke, tough!

Sarah

Magical

When you're in the job as long as I am, and you see some babies that are born to parents that never planned it and don't particularly want it, it's still magical, that minute of birth is still magical, to them and to me. But the real beauty, completely, is when you see people who really and truly have looked forward to this baby and have prepared for it and planned for it and you know they are going to do their very, very best to bring that child up to the best of their ability. That's when I can still cry. The father will be there crying, and I will cry. I will still cry, because it is just magical.

You're Irish

You will get the odd comment, "Oh, you wouldn't understand that, you're Irish," or stupid little things like that. If you had any sense at all you just let it go. It's not worth commenting on, and it probably wasn't meant with any seriousness. And if you took it up, you were just making a fool of yourself, I think.

The same experience

I think the Polish are having the same experience as the Irish did. There's an awful lot of Polish people coming into this country now. And if you look at them, they're white, they're Catholic, and English is not their first language and they have never had anybody to stand up for them.

There's a lot of Polish people going into Ireland as well to work for the very minimum wage, or below the minimum wage, like it or lump it. They're living in very poor quality housing, the same as the Irish did all those years ago.

Like little Barbie dolls

It was the time of Riverdance and Michael Flatley, and we saw it on the television. I think Niamh really and truly thought she was going to be up on the stage with a tiara. So she pestered me, and I asked around, did a bit of research on which was the least competitive Irish school of dancing. It's wicked, I think it's all wrong. It is cut-throat competitiveness and it's very, very costly. A girl that worked with me, she worked out, and this is at least ten years ago, that in a year she was spending probably in the region of £3,000 on her daughter's dancing. Now that daughter has now gone to university and never again will she put on a dancing dress or a pair of dancing shoes. But Niamh went to the dancing class for half an hour, and she came out, and she said, "It's not my kind of dancing." So I was quite glad because there is no way round it. You have to buy the shoes, you have to buy the dresses, you have to enter the competitions. And the wigs are completely naff, I think they're awful! They're all exactly the same, like little Barbie dolls. And the fake tan and the lipstick and the make-up! They're only tiny children. It's almost like the American beauty pageants. I think it's all gone too far. And we learned Irish dancing when we were at primary school. We paid like, a few bob to the dancing teacher, but she just taught you the steps in the classroom. And that's the way it should be. That's the way your culture is handed down to you.

Tom

Tom was born in 1935 in County Mayo. He first arrived in Leeds in 1953, returning to Ireland twenty years later to build a house for himself and his family.

The thing was, the English people was lovely and they knew what a day's work was. Whereas the Irishman wanted you to do a day and a half for him in the one day. Do you follow me now? That is a fact.

The ganger men

I worked with Murphy's, we were the chain gang with Murphy's. They called them the ganger men you know. And we were up on the Wakefield Road. But there was a gang there and they all went wrong. And they used to get the money you know, to pay digs and there were plenty of rooms you know, cheap digs and everything. There were regimental lads working hard and they'd have a few drinks but kept themselves decent you know, but these boys, no matter what you did with them, they'd just drink the money and sleep out at night. I've actually seen them sleeping in the graveyards in Wakefield Road until the police got sick of them and the neighbours complained about them you know, maybe urinating at the side of the road, things like that. But anyway, that was the craic in them days. They wouldn't look after themselves so I have not much sympathy for a lot of them, you know what I mean. They got the money and they spent it. We could have done the same couldn't we? We could have done the same. I won't say no more about it. That was the craic with them.

A good craic

I could make myself at home no matter where I went. No matter where I went I could always get on with people and have a good craic. Yes, yes. I mostly worked with English people when I was in England in my time. It's all English people here now you know, working. Wherever you go now. We had our turn, so it's their turn now, but. There's lot of English people retired here you know. There isn't a house, an old house round the place but they haven't bought.

Tom

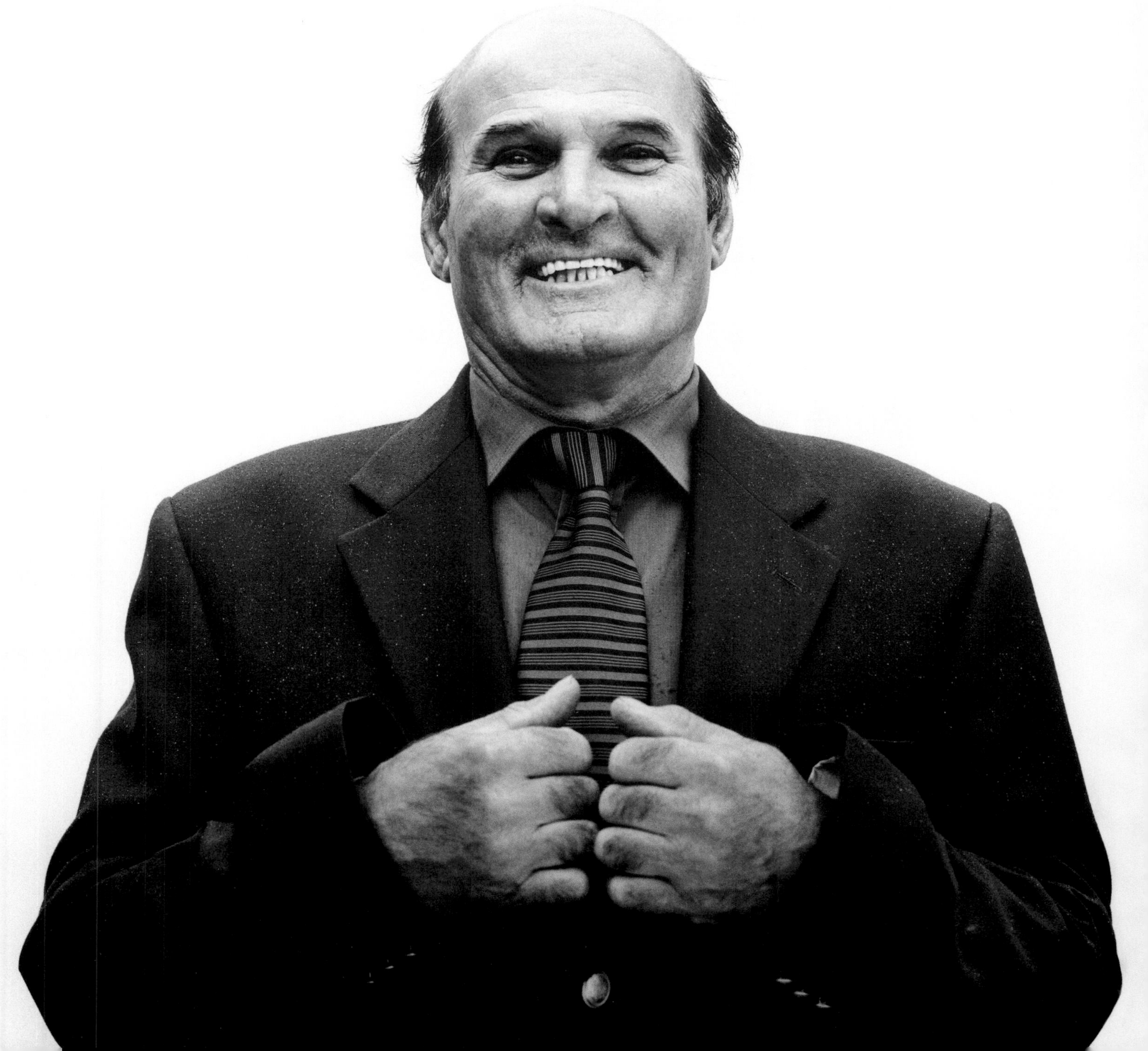